How to Be Rich By Using Other People's Brains, Time & Energy

STEPHEN COURAGE

HOW TO BE RICH BY USING OTHER PEOPLE'S BRAINS, TIME & ENERGY
Copyright © 2023 by Steve Courage

ISBN: 979-839-035-9464

All rights reserved. No part of this book may be reproduced, transmitted, or stored in a retrieval system, in any form or by any means, without permission.

LAYOUT & COVER DESIGN BY:
Busayo Lawrence
Email: support@busayolawrence.com
Website: www.busayolawrence.com

CONTENT

The Introduction *(02)*
Section One: The Only Way to Wealth *(04)*
Section Two: Discovering The Opportunities to Use Other People's Brains *(61)*
Section Three: Staying Focus While Building Your Empire *(106)*
Section Four: The Hands You Can Use *(144)*
Section Five: Starting The Process of Using Others Brains *(177)*

INTRODUCTION

There are millions of people all over the world who are dependent. These are people who wish other people or government institutions should solve their financial problems.

These people are the majority and they are obviously on the wrong side. But what about the independent people, people who believe in themselves and depend so much on themselves?

They too are (unfortunately) wrong!

Here comes the third group of people, people who are not dependent non independent, people who are interdependent.

While dependent people depend on other people or organisations to make them successful and independent people depend on their own self, their own hands, brains and energy to make them succeed in life, interdependent people stand in-between.

Interdependent people know that nobody can help them yet, they know that they can't help themselves either. Interdependent people believe so much in their own self but they master the art of working with other people, to use the brain, time, hands and energy of other people.

More than 95% of the world's people are either dependent or independent, which is a wrong path.

This book is about how to join the top 5% of people who become successful. This book is about interdependence.

This book is about how you can leverage on other people's brains, time, energy and resources to be rich and successful in a legitimate way.

Let's get started!

SECTION ONE
THE ONLY WAY TO WEALTH

This section has five chapters. My goal in this section is to show you that the ONLY way you can ever be wealthy is to master how to use other people's brains, time and energy.

My goal in this section is to take you to the point of concentration and (maybe) a little desperation that will help you to be rich.

CHAPTER 1
THE BIGGEST SECRET OF WEALTH

In September 2017 I had the privilege of hosting one of my business teachers, Mr Bukola Odedeji, at my residence in Lagos. He came visiting with his nine-year-old son, named Bishop.

Bishop is an inquisitive young boy whose father wishes he could grow up to be an entrepreneur.

On the second day of their visit, while we were in my office, Bishop asked, "What are you doing here?" "This is my company", I replied the curious boy.

"What do you do here?" Bishop asked.

After spending some time to explain the company's business model to Bishop (in a language a nine-year-old could understand), I now had before me the task of teaching him a business lesson.

"You see, Bishop", I started, "As you grow up, your goal should be to employ 25 people before you're 25 years old".

With amazement Bishop asked me, "Why must I employ 25 people, to pay salaries and share my money with them; the money I should spend alone?"

An outburst of laughter ensued in my office as his dad and I laughed to the young boy's ignorance.

Since ignorance isn't stupidity, I had to continue with my nine-year-old business student.

"You see, Bishop", I said as I thought of the best way to teach this nine-year-old that employers DON'T 'give' money to their employees, "You aren't going to be the one to 'give' money to your employees".

I immediately remembered that his mum produces and markets *Zobo*, a drink made from Hibiscus plant; so I decided to use that as an illustration.

"Imagine your mum employs 10 people to sell her *Zobo* drink daily", nodding, Bishop was expecting the next statement, "Each of these 10 employees of your mum sells ₦100 worth of *Zobo* daily" (I needed to use a very small amount to teach a 9 year old boy, you know?).

"Since your mum uses ₦70 to produce the 'Zobo' each of her employee takes to the market, she makes profit of ₦30 every day on every employee but pays each of them ₦20 as their wage", nodding his head to show he got the picture I was painting, I asked Bishop, "How much does your mother make every day from her 10 employees?"

Bishop is obviously not good in Maths so he needed to use his fingers to calculate ₦10 multiplied by 10 employees. "₦100", he excitedly announced after calculating.

Looking to his eyes to be sure he got the lesson, I asked Bishop "Do you understand now?"

He seemed to have understood partially part but I needed him to get the picture very clearly; so I asked, "How much does each employee of your mum make in this example?"

"₦20", my student replied.

"How much does your mum make?"

"₦100", Bishop thoughtfully reiterated.

I paused for few seconds (to get the lesson in his head) and asked as I looked into his eyes, "Do you think your mum actually gives money to her employees?"

"No", Bishop replied with a smile.

Having noticed that the boy now understood the lesson I repeated my earlier challenge for him. "As you grow up, your goal should be to employ 25 people before you're 25 years, and 100 people before you're age 30".

This time around, Bishop was no longer confused, "Okay" he answered as he looked for a pen and paper to write down the goal I needed him to set.

The Most Important Business Lesson

The first business lesson anyone could learn has been learned by my nine-year-old business student.

Few months after, I got a report from Bishop's father that the young boy was still curious about the idea of employing 25 people before the age of 25 and how he could get that done.

Fortunately for Bishop, he still has 16 years ahead of him to figure it out.

Why Did I Start The Entrepreneurship Training for Bishop The Way I Did?

I don't know any better way.

You see, the most important lesson about wealth creation anyone can teach is, "**Learn How to Use Other People's Brains, Time & Energy**".

Figure out how to employ and make other people work with or for you and you'll have more money than you can ever spend in your entire life.

I know the concept of "using other people's Brains, time & energy" would sound unethical to many people but this book is about the reality.

There's difference between the ideals (the way we want things to be) and the reality (the way they are, indeed).

In an ideal world, 'A', 'B', 'C', 'D' would all be rich by their hands or by working for each other. Unfortunately, that doesn't happen anywhere in the history of the mankind.

In the real world, 'D' uses the hands and time of the A, B and C to be wealthy.

In an ideal world, the wealth of the world would be shared evenly. Unfortunately, that was never the case.

As at the time of writing this book, the 62 richest people in the world have the equivalent of 50% wealth of the entire world population.

The meaning of that is: the richest 62 people in the world have the same amount of money as 3.5 BILLIONs of others, in the same world.

The richest man in the world, as at the time of writing this book has more money than the entire Africa's annual budgets.

The ideal is different from the reality. I wish it wasn't so, but (unfortunately) it is so.

The good news is that, the more reality you understand, the less stress you'll have and the more success you'll have.

So, if you love the ideal, this book wasn't written for you. But if you want me to share the real life happenings with you and you'll like to approach the world the way it is, not the way you want it to be, you've come to a book that will change your life forever.

Who is Paying Who?

Bishop (my nine-year-old business student) was afraid of employing people because he thought the employers have the responsibility of paying the employees.

"Why do you want me to employ 25 people at the age of 25; spend the money I should spend alone for my employees' wages?" Bishop queried me.

But wait!

It's easier to forgive Bishop for his ignorance (because he's a little child) but what about adults who lack this simple understanding?

It's easier to overlook the ignorance of a nine-year-old kid who thinks it's employers who are paying the employees, but what about a 29 or 39 year old who believes the same lie?

There's a man I knew about 10 years ago who worked as a prison warder with the Federal Government of Nigeria.

We met in a public transport one evening and as we were discussing (and because the day happened to be the last of the month) he was talking to somebody who was unemployed and boastfully said, "Whether they like it or not (referring to his employer) they are now my debtor".

Over the years I've seen many people (especially employees) who believe that their employers are doing them a favour.

Till today, most people still believe that the employers are helping the employees. They still think that the employers are paying the employees (so it seems).

But it's NOT.

Let me explain the hidden truth…

You see, you are the one actually paying your employer.

Yes, employees are the ones actually paying the employers.

Remember my encounter with nine-year-old Bishop. Remember the story of how his mum employs 10 people to sell her *Zobo* drink.

Each of the 10 employees sells ₦100 *Zobo* every day and gets ₦20 wages out of the ₦30 profit on each of their sales.

The employees go home (happily) with ₦20 each while Bishop's mum goes home with ₦100.

The employees are happy because they've got 'good' job but Bishop's mum is happier because the employees are actually helping her to be rich.

They do the work but she owns the system, so she's got just a little profit from each employee to make her richer.

Can Bishop's mum do the work of 10 people? Would she have made that much if she had worked on her business alone?

Without her employees, Bishop's mum cannot be rich. So, who is paying who?

Our society makes children believe in jobs because it does appear as though, if you get a job, you've got a chance to get someone (your employer) to do you a favour.

Well, the opposite is actually the truth.

The employees are the ones paying the employers. Your employer isn't doing you as much favour as you're doing him.

My employees are the ones paying me 'salary', not the other way round.

If you're getting this understanding for the first time, blame school that deceived you to love 'good jobs'.

I have something even more important to show you in the above story, but to make my point clear here before jumping to another point, think about the following;

Aliko Dangote is the richest man on the Continent of Africa as at the time of writing this book. The question I love to ask you is; "Who made Dangote rich?"

Take a moment to think about this.

Imagine that Aliko Dangote wakes up one Tuesday morning and all his 26,000 employees resigned and nobody else is willing to work for him. What do you think would happen to Dangote?

Now you got the point.

Aliko Dangote is going to become poor, in two years or less, if he has nobody to work for him.

Microsoft (own by Bill Gates) had 127,104 employees as at July, 2014. What do you think would happen, if everybody working for Bill Gates resigned and he got nobody to work for him?

As of today, Walmart (own by Sam Walton) has 2.3 million employees. That's the reason Walton's family is one of the richest families in the world.

What do you think would happen if all 2.3 million Walmart's employees resigned and nobody worked for the company?

Google has 61,814 full-time employees; Facebook, 23,165 employees and Apple has about 116,000 employees.

What happens if all of these employees resigned and nobody wanted to work for these big corporations anymore?

What do you think will happen to me, if all my employees resigned?

I will crash, almost immediately because there's no way I can make good money without them because they oversee different aspects of my businesses.

What's the point I'm making here?

It's actually the employees who pay their employer's wages, not the other way round.

What happens when Aliko Dangote wakes up is, he thinks of his business. But that's not the secret of his wealth. The secret is, 26,000 other humans also think of the Dangote's business.

That's an enormous power.

By 9 am, Dangote is working in his office, but that's not the reason why he's rich. The reason why he's rich is because, as he's using his two hands and one brain, there are 52,000 other hands and 26,000 other brains working for him.

Aliko Dangote isn't rich because he works hard. Millions of people equally work hard but still remain poor. Dangote (and every rich person) becomes rich because he has figured out how to legitimately use other people's energy and time to become rich.

Whether you think this is ethical or not is not the point here. The point is, that's how it is (and I'll soon prove to you that using other people's time and energy is both legitimate and holy)

Why Do I Expose This Hidden Secret?

I'm exposing this ugly truth because; the reason most people love jobs is because they see it as an easy way to live.

"Just go to work, 9am -5pm, 22 days in a month and get paid", they think.

Because school and the society has brainwashed most people, they believe the lie that the employers are paying the employees.

I'm convinced if every young African knows the truth that the employees are the ones paying the employers, most of them would have dreamed big and fought for financial freedom.

We all love to rush to where we'll be paid and that's why people rush to get jobs. What happens if people know that rushing to get jobs means THEY are going to pay their employers (rather than being paid)?

Do you ever wonder why wages and salaries are paid after (and not before) you've worked?

Just as it's in the case of Bishop's mum, she needs to get paid by her employees first, before she'll give them a part of the money THEY have given her.

Now that you've understood this hidden game, let's continue by visiting Bishop's story again.

When I got the responsibility to teach the nine-year-old Bishop entrepreneurship, why was figuring out how to employ people the first challenge I posed before him?

The answer is very simple. If you want to teach anybody how to be rich, the very first truth you'll let him know is that, nobody has ever become rich by working hard with his two hands and one brain.

Anyone who understands this truth will stop pursuing the wind (because you'll be pursuing the wind if you feel you can be rich as an employee).

On January 21, 2017, a friend told me that they had embarked on an industrial action (strike) at his place of work. While probing the reason for the strike, he said, "So many foolish reasons. One is that the employees want their retirement age to be 65, instead of 60 years".

The reason these people are fighting the government to extend their retirement age to 65 is because they are afraid of poverty.

These employees think if they could work five more years, they could be better financially.

If they knew that it doesn't matter how hard or how many years you worked; you cannot be rich by using your two hands and a single brain to make money, they would have fought with their inner self and not the government.

So many young people today are pursuing the wind by looking for 'good jobs', thinking if they got one they could be rich.

Today, so many adults are pursuing the wind by thinking, "If I can get a better job or work till 65, I can be better financially".

Don't be deceived.

If you like, work 20 hours daily for 50 years, you cannot be rich, until you learn how to legitimately use other people's hands and brains.

Anyone who understands this principle will ask the next question;

How Can I Use Other People's Hands & Brains, Legitimately?

Of course you won't go to the radio stations or newspaper houses to announce that you need 5,000 hands to be rich.

You'll have to employ these hands.

And yes, you won't go to the TV to announce that you want to employ 10,000 people because you want to be rich right away.

You can't employ people, trying to use other people's hands and brains, by just letting them resume to your office by 9am and return home by 5pm.

You have to engage these hands and brains in productive tasks; tasks that could pay their wages and yours in multiple fold.

For you to be able to employ someone you'll pay ₦100,000 monthly, his contributions to your business must worth ₦150,000 or more.

By the time you employ 100 of these brains, giving you ₦50,000 monthly (on average) from their hands and brains, then you have a ₦5 million monthly business.

To make your journey easier, you don't even have to employ one hundred people to reach the above goal. You can 'employ' few technologies that could do the jobs of 70 men. That means you'll employ just 30 human beings.

But (as I said earlier) you won't employ people to literally use their hands.

The meaning of this is that, there must be a lucrative product or service to be sold.
Yes, your end goal is to use other people's hands and brains to be rich but you can't just do that.

You must start from the foundation.

You must figure out a problem, create a product or service to solve this problem lucratively, then, you can employ two or five hands to sell such product or service.

From five employees, you can get to 10, 20, 50, 100 etc. employees, then, you'll be extremely rich because hundreds of hands are now working for you.

The formula looks so simple but confusing to so many people.

But, wait; I have your interest at heart.

Other parts of this book will be about other things you must do, to create a lucrative business that will allow you to employ tens and hundreds of people, so you'll become rich by using other people's hands and brains. But for now in this chapter, I'll try and make it very clear that you can never become rich, until you figure out how to use other people's hands and brains.

The Rich in History

Because I don't want you to read this book and think I'm simply making it up or making untrue claims, I'll like to take you down memory lane, to show you those who have been rich in the past and how they became rich.

If you knew how those who have been wealthy in the past became wealthy, you'll know how to become wealthy, too.

Because I'm a Christian and a student of the Bible, and because Bible gives us one of the earliest historical accounts of mankind, I'll prefer to start my analysis from the Bible.

The Bible speaks about few rich people – Abraham, Isaac, Esau, Job and David.

Let's see how these people made their money.

The first man Bible uses the word, "rich" to qualify was the Abraham. How did Abraham become very rich? Genesis 14: 14 tell us that Abraham had 318 slaves.

How Abraham became very wealthy is no science.

Whenever Abraham woke every morning, there were 318 other brains and 636 hands to work for him.

Why won't he become rich?

If as you wake up tomorrow you have 300 brains and 600 hands that work for you, would you be poor?

When you woke up this morning, how many brains went to work for you?

If 5, 10 or 20 brains do not work for you, how then do you want to become rich, like Abraham who had 318 brains to work hard for him?

Jacob and Esau are the next people the Bible uses the word "rich" for.

In Genesis 33: 1, the Bible tells us that Esau had 400 slaves and in the same chapter, we see the picture of Jacob's hundreds of slaves.

Why are these brothers (Jacob & Esau) so rich?

The answer is very simple.

No. They didn't work 23 hours daily. They didn't lie to get money or cheat to be rich.

They figured out how to legitimately use other people's hands and brains to become rich.

How many hands do you have working for you as you read these words?

If you only work with your two hands, how can you ever become wealthy?

Job was considered (in the Bible) as the "richest man from the East".

How did Job make his money? By working 20 hours every day or by working for 65 years?
None of the above!

Bible tells us Job's secret in chapter one of the book of Job.

It was very simple (though not easy). Job had hundreds of slaves who took care of his cattle, horses, etc.

David had been a shepherd since he was a boy and as a king, he had hundreds of slaves he probably used for his cattle rearing and other businesses.

Solomon inherited his father's business and continued using other people's hands and brains; that made him one of the richest men in the world.

Forgive me if you're not a Christian or you hate the Bible.

I needed to prove my point and that's why I visited one of the oldest books of history, the Bible.

The truth is; there is nobody called "rich" in the Bible who didn't use other people's hands and brains.

I've proven that and you can search the Bible yourself to confirm my claims.

Now let's move away from the Bible.

Mansa Musa of Mali was the richest man in the world in the 14th Century. He was worth about $400 billion (if his wealth was to be converted to today's currency)

Mansa Musa became very rich by having a company that dealt in Mineral resources like Salt, Gold etc. Because he had a business that sold products, he could easily use other people's hands and brains.

Jakob Fugger of Germany was the richest man in the 15th Century. He was worth $275 billion (in today's currency). He became rich by figuring out how to use other people's hands to build his banking and finance services business.

Suleiman, The Magnificent of Turkey was the richest man in the 17th Century. He was worth $100 billion (in today's currency). Suleiman became wealthy by figuring out how to use other people's hands, to run his Mineral resources company.

Stephen Girard and the Rothschild Family were the richest people in the 18th and 19th Century. They didn't become wealthy by working 24 hours every day.

They became wealthy by figuring out how to use other people's brains, time and energy.

The lesson here is very simple.

Different people from different generations have been wealthy through different means, but one thing remains constant – they all used other people's hands and brains.

Abraham in the Bible became very rich through cattle business, Rockefeller became rich through oil and Mark Zuckerberg became rich through social media.

These are entirely different ventures, yet, they all have one thing in common – they became wealthy by using other people's hands and brains.

Conclusion to Chapter One;

The purpose of this chapter is to open your eye to the reality about the game going on in the financial world, so that you'll not be a victim.

I started by telling you the first business lesson I taught Bishop (my 9-years-old business student) about business.

I made it very clear to you that, you can never become rich, until you figure out how to use other people's brains and hands.

I think this is very important for you to understand because if you did, you'll stop pursuing the wind.

If you understand this principle, you'll become desperate enough to build your own business empire that will allow you to use other people's brains and hands.

I also believe that the reason most people love being employed is because they were deceived to believe that it's their employers who are paying them. If I can get you to understand that employees are the ones paying the employers, you won't want to become a victim since everybody loves to be paid but hates to pay, you'll strive hard to position yourself where you'll be paid.

That's the purpose of writing this chapter. But this is just the beginning of this book.

I promise to show you how to use other people's brains and hands in a practical sense as we move on through this book.

For now, know it for certain that you can never become wealthy by using your two hands and one brain.

But should you have some doubts, read the next chapter…

CHAPTER TWO
KILL OR BE KILLED

I was speaking on phone with one of my company's prospective clients in the year 2017 when he told me the story of when he was a soldier.

According to him, their motto then was, *"For Peace to Rain, Blood Must Flow"*

An average military person consciously understands this. For peace to rain, blood must flow.

Just imagine you're going to the battle field, what do you think would be in your mind?

"I'll kill someone or someone kills me", I guess.

While the above is a very harsh example, I think it does communicates my point.

Some people will read the title of this book and hate me, some will stop at chapter one while some will even read the entire book to increase their hatred for my person.

"How can someone teach 'How to Use Other People's Brains and Hands to Be Rich?", they'll ask angrily.

If you've read the first chapter of this book and feel like, "Why should I use other people's time and energy?", then you must be ready for your time and energy to be used for 35 years.

It's that simple.

There's no third option. You can't sit on the fence.

You'll either be in or out.

If you cannot take the pain to learn how to use other people's hands and brains to build your wealth, you must be willing to sell your own hands and brain, for other people to use, to build their own wealth.

In other words, if you hate the idea of using other people's brains to be rich, you must love the idea of selling your own brains for someone else who want to be rich.

If the idea of using other people's time and energy to be rich sounds unethical to you, does the idea of selling your time and energy for someone else to be rich sound so good?

You obviously cannot stand on the fence.

You'll either learn how to be rich by using other people's brains and hands or you'll sell your own brain and hand for someone else to be rich.

This chapter is very important in order to get you desperate.

When I look around the continent of Africa, I see too many young people who are not passionate about anything.

I see too many adults who complain about everything, just as if complaining about such things would change them.

The reason this is so is because these people are not desperate enough to pursue their dreams.

One major reason people are not desperate is because they think they could sit on the fence and 'luckily' become rich.

Most people were simply deceived by the school and the society. This makes them to believe, "If I can just get a good job in a big company, I'll be fine".

If only these people know that they are planning to sell their hands and brains for penny, they would fight to pay the price to be on the other side of the coin.

When I was growing up as a young boy, I knew I was either going to pay the price to build my own company and make millions or work hard for another man's company and retire poor.

I knew I could not stand in-between and that gave me the courage to pay the price.

This chapter is about getting you to pay the price.

If I can get you to understand that you cannot get the third option, that you'll either buy someone's hands and brains or sell yours, you'll be passionate about building your own company.

Would you either buy other people's hands and brains, to make you rich, or sell your two hands and brain and die poor?

But Wait!

Entrepreneurs obviously buy other people's hands and brains to build their own wealth and employees obviously sell their hands and brains for penny.

But Steve, what about self-employed individuals?

Let's discuss that in the next chapter.

CHAPTER 3
WHY I HATE BEING SELF-EMPLOYED

Sometime around year 2009 I heard the governor of my state (Osun State, Nigeria), advising the young graduates posted to the state as part of their mandatory one year national service. "You see," he said, "now that you've finished school, make sure you're self-employed because there's no job anywhere".

If you listen to the radio or watch television today, such advice is everywhere.

I have two problems with this advice.

The first problem I have with the advice of being self-employed is that, if we as adults know that there's no job anywhere, why do we still train our children to be employees?

I mean, to me, that's a high level of deception.

We send these precious souls to schools and teach them how to be employees for 18-25 years. Now after they're filled with great expectations about the 'good jobs', we're advising them to be self-employed.

How does that make sense to anyone?

Why do we train them to be employees since we know there's no job anywhere?

The second problem I have with the advice of "be self-employed" is that, selfemployment is not sexy.

Self-employment is odd and boring.

No one has ever become rich by being self-employed because self-employment is still a job.

The only difference is that, self-employed people give themselves the jobs.

Instead of it to be better than a job, self-employment is even worse than being an employee.

Take for instance, if you're an employee, you'll work about 8 hours every day. But as a self-employed individual, you can work 12-14 hours every day.

Employees work 5 days each week. Many self-employed individuals work 6 or 7 days each week.

Employees receive their wages, whether their employers do well or not. Self-employed people don't get money if their businesses don't make sales.

Employees are entitled to annual vacation, but self-employed individuals aren't.

So what's exciting about being self-employed?

I am of the opinion that we should stop teaching our children how to be employees.

I also feel we should never advise them to be self-employed.

Don't be self-employed. Be an entrepreneur.

The Difference Between an Entrepreneurs and a Selfemployed Individuals.

Entrepreneurship and self-employment aren't the same.

Every entrepreneur creates a product, service or a better way of selling things. Selfemployed individual rarely do any of the above.

Every entrepreneur has a business system, a system that works for them, even when they sleep. Self-employed individuals have no system, so they must work for every penny they earn.

If all my above points don't seem to make much sense to you, the next point will;

Entrepreneurs have businesses that are scalable, businesses that could be in seven or 70 locations and running at the same time. You ever see any self-employed person having a scalable business?

That's the reason self-employed people can't be rich. They don't have a business system, they don't have scalable business, and they are not using other people's hands and brains.

You don't want to be self-employed and you don't want to advise anyone to be.

Small Business & Self-employment

Did I hear you say "But, Steve, everyone has to start somewhere"?

Yes, everyone has to start somewhere. Every business starts small, usually with one man or two men.

However, the big difference between a small business and a business run by selfemployed individual is the mind-set of the owner.

Even when I ran my business alone, I knew I was not self-employed. I knew I was building a company. I knew I must have a business system. I knew I must make my business scalable. I knew I must start using other people's hands as soon as possible.

I ventured fully into the business world in July, 2008 and six months after, I interviewed the first set of people I wanted to employ. I employed my first set of employees in January, 2009.

About seven months after, I had three employees and since then, I've always been on the lookout for whom to employ and partner with.

And guess what?

I didn't have money then; I was broke and my business wasn't doing well. But because I knew within myself that I was never going to be self-employed, I always looked for hands and brains to use.

That's the difference between the entrepreneurs and the self-employed individuals.

Self-employed people want to work harder; entrepreneurs want to build business systems that can work hard for them.

Self-employed individuals want to do it all by themselves. Entrepreneurs want to do it by using other people's hands and brains.

Another big difference is that, **quite often, entrepreneurs focus on how to sell things while self-employed people focus on how to make things**.

Let me explain this in details…

CHAPTER 4
LEARN HOW TO SELL THINGS; NOT HOW TO MAKE THEM

Sometime ago, my company worked with an agency of the Lagos State Government to train some youths in a skill acquisition program.

I and my team rendered services in this program as entrepreneurs (Entrepreneurs are people who sell you what you want, not necessarily what you need).

After this program however, I wrote to the appropriate office to explain to the authority, what I thought these young people actually needed.

You see, **you don't need to know how to do stuffs**. All you need to know is how to sell them.

I see so many people getting busy learning how to make bread, how to make soaps, how to make beads, how to sew clothes, how to repair laptops etc.

These people are busy doing the wrong things and the reason is because, that's what the government and the society is promoting.

Government is promoting "Skills Acquisition Programs" because they don't know better.

While knowing how to do one or two things isn't a bad idea, the more things you know how to do the poorer you'll become.

You don't need to know how to do or make things. You only need to know how to sell them.

Thomas Barratt said: **"Any fool can make soap. It takes a clever man to sell it."**

Take a moment to think about that!

Why would you waste your time, learning how to do what a 'fool' can do, since if 'fools' can do it, thousands of people will do it?

Why don't you spend time to learn what only the clever can do, since if it's for the clever, only few people will qualify?

Don't waste your energy learning what anybody can do. Learn what most people can't do – selling.

Let me give you some practical examples.

Jack Ma is the richest man in China (as at the time of writing this book). He owns the biggest E-commerce business in the entire continent of Asia, but you know something? He doesn't know anything about technology. According to him, his knowledge is limited to the use of e-mail and Google search.

All technical aspects of running an e-commerce business are handled by engineers. He focuses on are the real work – thinking, creating ideas and selling.

Henry Ford became one of the richest in the 20th Century by developing the engineering methods of mass production of automobiles.

But guess what?

Henry Ford was never an engineer. In fact, he spent just about eight years in school, so how could he be an engineer?

Though Henry Ford didn't know how to make automobile engines that revolutionized the automobile industry, he definitely knew how to 'use' other people's brains to do it.

He employed smart engineers and motivated them to get the work done.

The biggest work Ford did was the work of thinking. That's why he later said, **"Thinking is the hardest work"**.

Yes, thinking is the hardest work and that should be your work.

You shouldn't concentrate your energy on how to make stuffs. You should concentrate your mind on how to sell them.

Dangote became a billionaire through the cement business. Do you think he knows everything about how to make cement?

He probably knows just a few things. But he knows how to build a business system and how to sell.

In 2017, Dangote began building an oil refinery in Nigeria. You'll be wrong to think Dangote knows about the technical part of building and operating a refinery.

Entrepreneurs are not people who know how to do things. They are people who focus on how to discover human wants, gather people who know how to DO, and create a business system to sell their products and services profitably.

In March 2017, my agriculture technology company rented a place in Lagos for our business operations. As it's the custom, the landlord of the property asked me, "What are you guys doing?" "We're an agriculture consultancy company", I explained.

Few weeks later, three gun wielding policemen stormed our office with intent to arrest 'criminals' (who they thought were myself and my employees).

We latter suspected our landlord to be the informant and the reason is very simple; we told him that we were agriculture-related company but we never brought a cutlass or hoe, so he assumed that we must be up to something fraudulent.

Well, Uber is a transportation company but Uber has no cab.

Now, my agriculture technology company is based in Lagos but has operational presence in more than 21 states of Nigeria, yet I can't recall the last time I held a cutlass or a hoe.

Don't learn how to do stuffs. Master how to build a business system that sell stuffs.

If you ever want to be rich, you'll not be busy learning how to make bread, how to make soaps, etc. You'll concentrate on how to discover what people want and how to sell what they want for them. You can always hire other people to make anything.

This is another secret of wealth creation. **Don't waste much time learning how to make things. Learn how to sell things instead.**

McDonald is not the best burger maker in the world. So many people all over the world know how to make burgers but they don't know how to build a business so they are poor.

Coca-Cola isn't necessarily the best beverage in the world. The best drink may be in your city, in the hand of someone who doesn't know how to build a business.

Close-Up and Oral-B are not necessarily the best toothpastes in Africa, but they are in the hands of the entrepreneurs.

The best toothpaste brands could be in the hands of a scientist in your state and nobody will ever know about it because he or she is a doer, not a seller.

"Any fool can make soap. It takes a clever man to sell it." – Thomas Barratt

When next you hear anybody talk about "skill acquisition", don't pay attention because any average man can make soap but only smart men sell soap for profit.

You think about it.

Thousands of people are making bread in your state, hundreds of people are making soaps in your country and hundreds of people claim to be good cooks in your city, but only very few people ever built successful soap, bread or restaurant businesses.

The reason is because most people have been deceived to focus on "skill acquisition" which means, "Learn to make things".

You must learn how to sell things.

What Do I Expect From You?

If you truly want to be rich by using other people's hands and brains, you can't do that by being a doer. You must be a seller instead.

You must focus on how to discover human wants and how to sell things at profit.

When most people want to venture into business, what they are looking for is a product to sell to make money.

Don't focus on which products to sell. Focus on HOW to sell to make millions.

Focus on marketing. Focus on learning what makes human beings to buy and design your own business to make people want to buy from you.

Be a student of market. Study marketing, human psychology and branding.

If you want to be rich by using other people's brains, if you want to build a great business empire, you must not focus your energy on how to make stuffs. You must focus on how to discover what people want and how to sell your company's products to hundreds of thousands and millions of people.

People who know how to make stuffs end up selling their brains to people who know how to sell stuffs!

Learn how to sell things and not how to make them and you'll discover that money isn't scarce.

Or do you think money is scarce?

CHAPTER 5
WHO SAYS MONEY IS SCARCE?

As a young boy growing up in the village, I had to say some special prayers before I'll asked my father for money.

I became so afraid of him that my heart would beat so fast, as though the judge of a law court was about to pass down a sentence.

On such occasions, my father's default response would be, "Where is the money?"

You probably had a similar experience because we all live in a society where most people believe that money is scarce.

Well, if you want to build wealth, you must not join them in believing such trash.

Nothing in the world is scarce, not even money.

Every scarcity humans experience is artificial scarcity.

Nothing in the world is scarce.

Think about this for a moment. Prior to the 1958, Nigeria believed that crude oil was a very scarce commodity (because the country didn't know she had oil buried beneath).

After the oil was discovered, Nigeria became the 5th oil producing country.

Was oil truly scarce in Nigeria before the 1958?

No. It was abundant, but no one saw it.

Up till today, many countries of the world are still discovering crude oil.

Is that crude oil just getting there? No. It has been there thousands of years but nobody saw it.

Drinkable water is very scarce in some parts of the world and many would believe that water is actually scarce.

But wait. Water covers about 70% of the entire planet Earth. How then can water be scarce? Blame humans (not God) for the lack of water in the world.

We can believe that Gold, Silver or Diamond is scarce, until more attention is paid into searching the world for them.

In fact, a closer look at Diamond revealed that it became scarce because it was hoarded by some devilish entrepreneurs.

Africa is one of the poorest parts of the world but you know something?

The natural resource in Africa (including diamonds, gold, iron, cobalt, uranium, copper, bauxite, silver, petroleum, etc.) is sufficient to take care of the entire world.

How come Africa is poor?

God gives humans everything in abundance but we have the right to believe we have nothing and we shall have nothing.

God created everything in abundance but we can decide to believe anything is scarce and it shall be scarce for us.

Nothing in the world is scarce, not even money.

Listen!

How can anyone say money is scarce when more than $4 trillion roam the world every day?

I mean, more than **4 TRILLION dollars** move around the world every day, looking for who to take them.

Every day, more than 4 trillion dollars move from some hands into another's hand and there's no law under the Sun that forbids you from taking any part of this enormous amount.

The only law is; *Ask and it shall be given!*

"Steve, O. Courage is definitely crazy!"

"If it's just to ask for it, why can't everyone be wealthy?"

Well, it's just to ask for it, but money doesn't understand English, French, Arabic or whatever your language is, so if you call the money with your human language it will simply not answer you.

Service, Service, Service. That's the only language money understands.

Money isn't scarce. You can command all the dollars you ever need and much more, if only you can speak the language which money understands.

Service is the name of that language.

You don't get what I mean?

Listen to what ZigZiglar said;

> **"You will get EVERYTHING you want in life, if you help enough other people to get what they want"**

You'll get all the money you want in life, if you'll help enough people to get what they want. Simple!

Money isn't scarce. Generosity is.

Money isn't scarce. Genuine love is.

The reason most people are poor is because they are stingy and have little or no love for their fellow creatures (but they won't believe this truth).

To command more than enough money into your life, you must be generous; you must (genuinely) love your fellow being.

"How, Steve?"

Well, you will get every money you ever need in life, if only you'll help enough people to get what they want.

This calls for love and generosity which our world doesn't preach. This is the service I earlier talked about.

Your goal in life is to attract to yourself only a tiny percentage of the $4 trillion that moves around the world every day.

To achieve this goal, all you have to do is serve fellow humans, then, they'll willingly give you the money.

How do you achieve this?

Through a product or service!

Human beings have so many problems and because these problems make life difficult for us, we're willing to solve them by giving away our money.

Because of this, whenever we find anyone who wants to help us to solve one of our problems, we joyfully give out our hard earned money. In return, this problem solver becomes richer.

Let me give you some very simple examples.

You spend money every day, right?

Now pause a moment to think about 10 things you've spent your money on in the last one month.

This exercise is very important so take a pen and list the 10 things you've spent money on in the last 30 days.

What are they?

First, they are either products (like toothpaste, call cards, food, etc.) or services (like public transport to your working place, your Cable TV subscription, electricity bill, etc.)

Second, all these things you paid for solved a problem for you, that is, you cannot surf the internet without data on your phone (a problem), so you bought 3GB data from your service provider (a solution that helps you to solve your problem).

Third, someone becomes richer because he or she helps you solve those problems with products or services.

All you have to do to make all the money you'll ever need all your life is to figure out how to do to others what the 10 products or services you listed above did for you.

Just as the 10 products or services you mentioned above helped you solve certain problems, you must figure out how to create a service or product to solve other people's problems.

If you do this tough job right, as you make different entrepreneurs richer every day (by giving them money), the more people you can help with your product or service, the richer you'll become.

You must love human beings enough to want to solve their problems and you must love yourself enough to make enough money from helping them. The first love is missing and that's the reason poverty is common.

One stressful night I was having a tough time in Ibadan, southwest Nigeria.

It rained and the dilapidated bus I boarded meandered waived through the bad sections of the road. I felt a great pain within my heart that night and said to myself, "I'm going to make a change in Africa, even if I'll sacrifice my life"

Since my adolescent, I've always looked for ways to solve problems.

Because of this eagerness to solve Africa's problems, I rejected the offer to process America Visa Lottery, even when I was just about 19 years old. To me, running away from Africa is a disservice to my Fatherland.

Because I am passionate about solving problems, I had to get my head thinking, experimented and failed severally before I could figure out how to do it right.

When next you hear anyone say, "There's no money", reply them, "There's no love either".

It's amazing how so many Africans hate their countries and love the United Kingdom and the United States of America. And you're wondering why we're still slaves? And you're angry that a white president called the African continent "shitholes"?

Don't blame him. Blame us all.

It's a 'sin' to say money is scarce. It's as good as pointing the accusing finger to God who has created everything in abundance.

Let no African go to the mountain to beg God for money. Let Africans stop fasting for 21 days to beg God for money.

Why should you beg your father to help pay your school fees, after he has given you the money to do so? That's irresponsibility!

Never say, "God, please make me rich," because God has already made you rich.

Instead, say, "God, please open my eyes to see human problems and the ideas to solve those problems profitably". (In the following chapter, I'll take you through how to discover human problems)

Africans should stop being foolishly religious. We should stop crying to God as if He hates us.

We should stop begging God to do for us, what we ought to do for ourselves.

It's not the duty of God to make us rich (because He has already made us so). It's by choice we're poor and we can choose to be rich, if we want to.

Don't ever believe that money is scarce because more than $4 trillion roam the world every day, looking for who to solve problems.

You need more money?

Increase your love for fellow humans, look for their problems and work hard to provide a creative solution (in form of a product or service), then smartly monetize your solution to make some millions.

When next you hear anyone say "Money is scarce!" tell them, "But over $4 trillion roam the world daily".

How can 4 trillions of anything be scarce?

How can you tell me that money is scarce while over $4 trillion walk the globe every day?

Money isn't scarce; problem solving skills are scarce.

SUMMARY FOR FIRST SECTION ONE

I started this section by announcing to you that you cannot be rich until you figure out how to use other people's time and energy.

I went far and deep to prove it, by giving you real life examples, even from the Bible and history.

Because I know you may still be sceptical about this immutable concept, I went further in Chapter Two to show you that a soldier will rather kill or be killed. You'll rather learn to use other people's time or you'll sell your own time for someone else to be rich.

I sure know you don't want to be a victim, if you can be a victor.

Chapter Three was designed to build on the Chapter Two. I know some people could think "I can be rich without using other people's time or selling mine. I'll just become self-employed", and that's what Chapter Three was designed to tackle.

In Chapter Three, I explained in detail that being 'self-employed' is still being an employee anyway and nobody can be rich being 'self-employed'.

Yes, everyone has to start small, but as I've explained, the mind set of being selfemployed is different from the mind-set of an entrepreneur with a small business.

In Chapter Four, I explained that you can't be rich by knowing how to make soap, how to make bread, how to rear chickens, etc.

This was to build on what I started in the Chapter Three (being self-employed) because people with self-employment mentality always think about how to make a product or service, not how to sell their services or products to millions of people.

I gave you examples, from Jack Ma to Dangote, to myself. Though rich people can know how to do things (for instance, Mark Zuckerberg knows how to code and Steve Job was a great designer), but deep within these guys is the selling skills which are far deeper than doing skills.

You can learn how to do one or two things but don't concentrate on that. Concentrate all your energy on how to market and how to sell your ideas, philosophy and products to millions of people.

"Any average man can make soap. It takes a genius to sell soap at profit"

You can always employ people to DO stuffs, so concentrate on how to sell things.

Though most people believe that money is scarce, Chapter Five, on the contrary showed that money isn't scarce.

Every day, more than $4 trillion exchange hands all over the world. This huge amount goes to people who ask for it, people who are able to solve human problems and creatively monetize their product and services.

Towards the end of this section, I know the question you're likely to be asking is, "How can I attract more money to myself?", "How can I discover human problems to solve and make much money, by using other people's brains, time and energy?"

That's exactly what the next chapter will show you.

But before you go to the next section of this book, I strongly recommend you go through this Section One over again.

The reason is because Section One of this book is the foundation. If you don't understand it very deeply, every other thing you want to read in this book may not make any sense to you.

So please, don't be in a hurry to go into the second section.

Kindly take your time to go through the first section (chapter 1-5) of this book again.

I Love You.

SECTION TWO

HOW TO DISCOVER THE OPPORTUNITIES THAT WILL ALLOW YOU TO BUILD THE EMPIRE, SO YOU'LL BE ABLE TO USE OTHER PEOPLE'S BRAINS, TIME & ENERGY

INTRODUCTION

My objective in the first section of this book is to reveal to you the secret everybody who has ever become rich knows and uses, the secret of using other people's brains, time and energy.

While I really need you to understand this concept, I as well want to simplify it.

Yes, you can only be rich if you can figure out how to use other people's time and energy. While this is the end, the means to the end must not be omitted.

While your goal is to figure out how to use 10, 100, 1,000 people's brains, time and energy in the nearest future, I owe you the responsibility of showing you how you can achieve that goal.

The formula looks something like; Look for a profitable problem to solve, understand a product or service that can solve such problem, employ people with different skills to create and sell such service/product and you'll be rich.

I've started this book with the end (using other people's time & energy) and I think I have to work you through the means (how to achieve the end).

"How can I discover business opportunities to build a business around, that will allow me to use other people's time & energy?"

That's what I'll be showing you in this section.

CHAPTER 1
LOOK FOR CHANGE, BUT THE RIGHT ONE

One day in February, 2018, I was with a friend and as we were having a nice time together, chatting about a whole lot of things, because my friend knows me to be a business genius (Pride. Lol), he asked me, "Why is comedy business booming these days?"

This was a man who understood that in the past, being a comedian was tantamount to being a beggar and a social outcast.

Now, he observed that many comedians these days are millionaires who make tons of money just from cracking jokes and he wished to know what's happening.

"It's about change", I explained to him.

It's about change in the economy.

In the early 70's and 80's, we had a fairly balanced economy. People were happier, families were more united, and parents didn't experience much financial headaches that would require a whole lot of thinking or waking up in the night to cry or sob.

As a result of this, husbands went to their works with clam, and returned to their wives and kids with excitement and happiness on their faces.

That time was much more peaceful. People didn't worry about much things.

Suddenly, things started changing. The economy began to deteriorate. People began to worry about their finance, marriage and security.

People's emotions started changing, and a lot of people began to show aggressiveness. People became sadder and unhappy. As people's happiness began to drain over the years, they began to look for artificial joy.

There comes a business industry, comedy. Comedy is an artificial joy but people are willing to pay for it.

Why? Because of the change that has occurred in our lives.

So many people are heartbroken today than ever before in history of mankind. Marital unfaithfulness, misbehaved children, financial crisis, insecurity are all problems that needs artificial joy to suppress and comedy is one of the easy solutions.

This is a change in our society, at the same time, a business opportunity for guys who are humorous and smart enough to discover it.

The above was the explanation I gave to my friend.

What's the lesson here?

Whenever you're looking for the opportunity to build a business that will allow you to use other people's brains, time & energy and make a lot of money, look for change.

Change and opportunity are brothers. They walk together. Whenever there's a change, there's an opportunity in-between the line.

If you lived in the 70's and you're fortunate to be alive to compare the living conditions of today, you'd discover that people don't have the same emotions.

Sometime in the year 2018, I listened to an interview with Femi Kuti (son of the late popular Fela Anikulapo Kuti). He talked about when he was growing up.

He grew up in Lagos where almost no one had fences surrounding their houses. He said people closed the door of their rooms when they wanted to retire to bed at night but they never closed the doors at the entrance to their houses. Imagine the Africa's centre of commerce, yet there wasn't fences in most people's houses.

But that's not the point. The point is that they didn't even close the doors to the entrance of their houses. They only closed the doors of their rooms to enjoy privacy especially for the married couples. At that time, not many people were after other people's life, cars or money.

Fast forward to the present time.

I live in Lagos (as at the time of writing this book) and you can hardly see a house without fences, except in very poor neighbourhood.

People now live with much more worries and anxieties and that's a change.

But that's not a good change, right? It really doesn't matter.

As every change brings opportunity, that change has led to products and services for some people.

We listen to comedy because we need artificial joy, artificial happiness.

Most of us need to get our laughter from comedy because our natural environments do not give us much reasons to smile anymore.

The political atmosphere of our country doesn't give us a reason to smile. Our spouses and extended family may not give us a reason to smile. Our jobs may not give us a reason to smile.

And since you want to smile and be happy, you're willing to pay for laughter, which is why comedians are becoming millionaires.

So, what am I saying here?

It doesn't really have to be a good change. Whenever you see a change, you see an opportunity.

Are you looking for the business opportunities that will help you to build a business which will allow you to use other people's brains and energy in your country?

Look for changes, but the right changes.

Now, so many people are expecting the wrong change while some people don't even know how to take an opportunity from a change.

So many people are expecting political change. That's what I call "the wrong change" because politics rarely change anybody's life.

Ben Carson said, "*We've been conditioned to think that only politicians can solve our problems. But at some point, maybe we will wake up and recognize that it was politicians who created our problems.*"

As a potential entrepreneur, don't expect a political change, except if that means you can get some government's contracts.

When people talk about political change, they're talking about the fact that they're tired of their current government and they feel that if another person comes into power, things are going to change drastically and they hope that if things can change, it's going to help them, it's going to improve their lives, it's going to make them wealthy.

As a smart individual, don't look for such change! If you're my student, and you're reading this book, don't wait for political change.

You're smarter than that!

An average man wants to believe that a political leader will solve most of his problems; which unfortunately, doesn't happen most of the time.

You're the one that can solve your problems. Therefore, look for the right change! Don't look for a political change.

Steve, how then can I see a change?

Let me give you another example to open your mind.

Sometimes in the year 2017, I was with two of my friends. We were talking about
Biafra (Biafra is a secessionist group in Nigeria)

As an entrepreneur, I asked my friends "What if Biafra eventually secedes from Nigeria?"

"How can we make some good money from such a change?", I asked as we started brainstorming.

Yes, secession isn't usually a good thing, but it's an opportunity because it's a change.

Every change brings business opportunities.

What do you think would happen if Biafra secedes today?

That is going to make some people become poorer, while some people will become richer.

People who become richer are going to be people who look for a profitable opportunity which the new change has caused.

These are people who ask, "What can this new country lack and how can we provide it?", "What policy is this new country likely to implement and how can we take advantage of that?", "What is this new government likely to favour with its agenda and how can we take advantage of that?", "What would this new government/country need and how can I provide some of these things profitable".

It's a change and it will bring opportunities.

You want to discover profitable opportunities in your country? Look for change.

Let me give you another example.

You read in the news that government has decided to move a major market in your city to another new location.

That's a change and it will bring opportunities for those who can think.

What if you go quickly to the new area to acquire some piece of land (Because rent would soon skyrocket in that environment) or you look for a way to position your small business in the new market?

When the economy gets bad, it's employees who get burnt by losing their jobs or by suffering from the inflation that has make their money less valuable.

Because entrepreneurs understand that change in the economy is nothing but an opportunity, they simply get busy looking for another line of business while employees are busy blaming anyone they think is responsible for their poverty.

If you'll ever become a successful entrepreneur, you must learn how to think different. You must learn how to see opportunities where everyone else sees crisis.

You think about this.

When you hear that there's war somewhere, you can be sure that two things are happening at that time.

The first is that there is a change, which is a bad change though. When there's war, a lot of people rush out of that zone because bad thing is happening right there.

The second thing you can be sure of is, most time, some people are going to that war zone.

Take for instance, when you hear that war starts in a city, so many people want to leave that city. Some of the people running out already have investments in that city.

But they don't care. All they are after is to sell their investments (properties etc.) and escape from that place before the war totally engulfs the place.

Then, you'd see some smart entrepreneurs coming in to buy these investments at very cheap prices. Why? Entrepreneurs know that while there might be war today, that war wouldn't last forever. Entrepreneurs know that war is a change; even though it's a bad one and that every change brings an opportunity!

Therefore, wherever you notice a change, look for an opportunity there!

Most of the examples I used in this chapter has something to do with negative change (From how unhappiness helps comedy business to how Biafra may make some people rich to how war could bring opportunity). This is good for you because you can now see that, even when things seems to be worse, opportunities for wealth creation are hidden somewhere.

Keep on looking for change, any change.

Change in human's emotional, physical or spiritual life are all opportunities.

Change in the ways women dress is an opportunity to create a clothing line and change in men's thinking about wrist watch could be another opportunity.

Never stop looking for change because there lies your opportunity for wealth creation.

While I'm sure this chapter's got you fascinated and excited about learning how to manufacture money, the next chapter will do much more!

CHAPTER 2

LOOK FOR PROBLEMS, BUT IN THE RIGHT WAY

In the year 2008, when I just launched myself fully into the business world, I had an habit of taking a pen and paper into a lonely place.

I would sit down and start thinking and writing business ideas.

What I was doing was looking for problems.

Every human being is concerned about problems. But unfortunately, 99% of people look for problems, not because they want to solve them, but because they want to complain about them.

That's the reason why when you look at your environment, whether in your office, or in public transport, you'd realise that people spend every of their free time to talk about problems.

Most people talk about problems to point fingers to A or to B, not to solve the problems. People complain every day, simply looking for whom to blame.

I don't blame people who spend all their life blaming others because that's what they were trained to do.

Most times, an average man grew up in a family where everyone complains about everything. So, it's just normal for them to complain. That's how their parents behaved too!

As an entrepreneur, you need to take another route.

Look for problems, not to complain about them, but to solve them profitably because problem is money.

Decide to be responsible

Naturally we grew up to complain about problems and put the blame on others. To me, that's irresponsibility which is the most terrible disease in the continent of Africa today.

Nobody wants to solve problems. Everyone looks up to someone.

An average African looks up to the government to solve his financial problems while an average Africa political leader looks up to the Europe, America, even Asia, to solve their problems.

Problem solvers are money manufacturers. That's why the US is rich, that's why the UK is fine, that's why China is doing well.

These countries have good numbers of citizens who wake up each morning to look for problems, not because they want to complain about them, but because they want to solve them.

In return, these people make several billions of dollars by thinking and creating products and services that solve the world's problems.

Just about a hundred years ago, the whole world was in total darkness. Some people solved that problem with the electricity and became wealthy.

Just a few years ago, the people in the world cannot communicate easily. Some people solved that problem with mobile phones and became wealthy.

Your clothes, shoes, cars, food, etc. are other people's creativity.

These people are able to create because they are responsible.

What the irresponsible people know how to do is to complain.

Look for problems, not to complain about it, but to solve it.

Stop looking for what the government of your country doesn't do, start looking for what you can do to solve some of the problems in your country.

I'm not saying it's easy to solve problems. I'm saying solving problems can make you extremely rich.

If you make it your responsibility to look for problems and to think about how you can solve them, you'll immediately see the need to get other people involve to form a synergy with you, to solve the problems you want to solve.

You may need to employ tens, hundreds or thousands of people as time goes on, to solve some of the problems your company want to solve.

That's what I call using other people's hands to be rich.

The bigger the problem you solve for people and the larger the numbers of people you can solve that problem for, the richer you'll ever be.

The richest men in our world are people who solve the biggest problems.

Till the 20th Century, human beings travel mostly through horses and chariots.

Even when automobile was invented, only the rich could afford them because there wasn't mass production of the automobile.

A guy without formal education rose from nowhere and worked hard to invent methods of mass production in the automobile industry.

The name of that guy was Henry Ford. He (needless to say) became the richest man in the world.

When computer was invented, it was a gigantic machines that could be as big as an entire room, very expensive and not accessible to most people of the world.

A young guy was concern about that problem and worked hard to solve it. His name is Steve Job. Job gave the world a small and affordable computer and became a billionaire, even before age 30.

Nigeria was importing almost everything, including cement. Aliko Dangote saw that as a problem (and it was).

Dangote started local manufacturing of cement and become the richest man in Africa.

Otunba Gandafi noticed that Nigerians are complaining about in-availability of public toilets in the early 90s. That was a problem.

The 30 years old Gandafi founded DMT mobile toilet and made his millions.

You want to be rich?

Look for problems.

Everybody who has ever become rich in the world, right from the time of Abraham, do so by solving one human problem or another.

If you understand this, you'll cry for most Africans.

An average African is complains about everything.

The reason is because most of us are not responsible.

See your country problem as your responsibility

If you'll ever become rich in your life, you must learn how to see your country's problems as your problems.

If you even want to be richer, you'll need to learn how to see your continent's problems as your problem.

You wish to become massively wealthy? Learn to see the world's problems as your problems.

If you see your country's problems as your personal problems, would you complain every day about it? Do you complain in the public transport about your marital headaches? Do you tell your co-workers about your child's failures in school? Rarely.

You don't cry in the public about your personal problems because you know it's your responsibility and it's up to you to solve it.

Stop crying about your country's problems. It's YOUR responsibility to solve them.

My life's goal is to solve as many problems as I can solve in the continent of Africa before I'll breath my last.

Most times, I don't even think about my country (Nigeria). I think about my continent, Africa.

Africa problems are my personal problems and my personal responsibility.

I decided to see it this way because I know money lives inside problems.

The rich are rich because they solve problems. The poor are poor because they complain about problems.

"But I can't solve some of my country's big problem", some people would tell me.

Yes, you cannot solve many problems but you can solve some. Look for those you can solve and never complain about those you don't have the capacity to solve yet.

"But Steve, I don't know how to see a problem", some people may say.

Every human needs and wants is a problem.

What people need and want, that's their problems.

Listen to what people complain about. Pay attention to how people behave. Think about what products or services you can provide better than those providing them today?

You want to be rich by using other people's hands and brains?

Look for people's problems you can solve, then use other people's hands and brains to solve those problems for thousands and hundreds of thousands of people.

That's how to be wealthy.

CHAPTER 3
LOOK FOR KNOWLEDGE, THE RIGHT ONE

A man in the 18th Century by the name James happened to be a stone seller. Stone sellers those days were people who break stones and sell them for those who wanted to build house.

One Saturday morning, Mr James went out to his business as usual, but this time around, James dig Diamond and packed them with the stone he was to go and sell.

On his way to go and sell Diamond (which he believed was stone), James met a Diamond expert who recognized immediately that what James carried wasn't just stones, but stones and Diamond.

As expected, the Diamond expert bought the entire load of "stone" from James and became a millionaire.

The above story was imaginary, yet, it all happens all the time in our world that stone sellers come across Diamond without knowing it.

Whenever I hear people talking about "great business idea", I know they actually don't know what they are talking about. Like Mr James in my above story, if you've not trained your mind to recognise Diamond, even if you see it, you'll simply think it's stone.

Like Mr James in my story, if you don't equip yourself, daily, with business education, even when the greatest business idea in the world come by your way, you'll either not recognize it or you'll mess the whole thing up within few months.

The American famous entrepreneur and musician Jay-Z said, **"I'm not a business man, I'm a business"**.

Nobody is a business man. We're all businesses.

You cannot be a business man. You can only be a business.

You can only build your business to the degree by which you've built yourself.

You can only earn as much as you've learned. The more you learn, the more you earn.

I'll write in details about the importance of daily learning but for now, let me get it registered into your mind that you have to seek knowledge, every day of your life, just as if it's oxygen. If you can't do this, you can simply go and get a job because you can't go far in the business world until you know so many things your competitors don't know and the only way you can know what they don't know is to seek knowledge, every day.

Diamond is everywhere but most people are stone sellers.

Until you train your mind to see Diamond, everything in the world looks like stone.

Business ideas are nothing. No idea can make you rich. People only become rich when they know what 99% of people don't know.

I'll go into details on this topic later inside this book.

CHAPTER 4
LOOK FOR PEOPLE, BUT THE RIGHT PEOPLE.

When we were in school, we did our tests and exams alone. To call your mates for help during the exams or tests is called cheating and you could be expelled out of the school for it.

After we have gone through this stupid programming for the first 20 years of our lives, it's just natural that we live the rest of our lives with that mind-set.

School is stupid and the reason is because it does more evil to the lives of children than good.

Today as I write these words, 99% of people I know still remain lone rangers victims, doing life's exams the way they do school exams and I don't blame them because they have been programmed to live that way.

In schools, asking for help during exams is call cheating. However, in life, trying to be rich all by your strength is stupidity.

This book is about how to be rich by using other people's brains, time and energy and I should have as well titled it, "Synergy".

You must understand synergy and make it your lifestyle.

You must learn how to "cheat" through life and by that I mean, you must learn how to work with people.

You must learn how to cooperate, collaborate and form team with other people, if you truly want to be rich and successful in life.

If you look at anyone who has become rich today, deep in their bones is the power to partner, collaborate and synergize with other people.

There's an innovative product call Lumos in Nigeria.

Lumos is a solar electric product that allows you to get a yellow solar box that can power your light, TV, Laptop etc. by you paying a monthly subscription for the box and the solar panel.

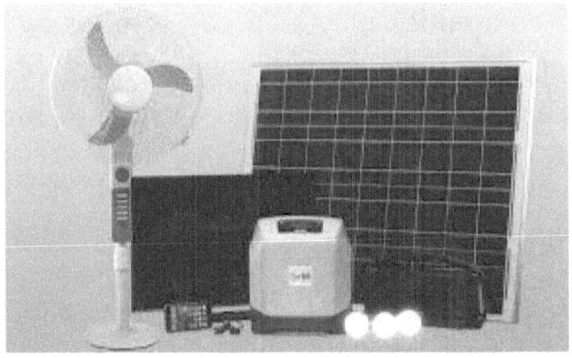

While I think this company is smart, I know quite well that they are not doing anything technically special. In fact, many other guys have been trying to do the very thing the Lumos guys are doing.

Lumos guys are only smart in one way and that was in collaboration.

Lumos is a separate company and has nothing to do with the MTN, but they look for the way to collaborate with the MTN and that changed everything else.

Lumos is being marketed under the MTN brand, giving the Lumos an hundred times more chance over their competitors. Lumos services can also be paid for via the MTN network, giving them another multiple power over their competitors who cannot easily get paid via call card.

Yes, Lumos will have to give certain percentage of their profit to the MTN, but 70% of a million dollars is bigger than 100% of one hundred dollars.

Cooperating, collaborating and partnering with other people and companies may lead you into losing 10-30% of your business but it's actually very smart because that single collaboration can triple your company's income.

Wistron is a big company that has employed more than 60,000 people all over the world. You know what they do?

Wistron Corporation makes ICT product for other companies to use in their names.

For example, if you buy an iPhone, you may think that Apple "made" that phone but you'll be wrong because many parts of that phone were actually made by an entirely different companies.

What Wistron does is to make parts of ICT products, like phone screens, laptop screens, etc, for companies like Apple, Samsung, etc.

As at the time of writing this book, Bill Gates is the richest man in the world. So many people know that Bill Gates became a billionaire by building the Microsoft, but what they don't know is, how it all happened.

In the year 1980, Microsoft was able to strike a partnership deal with the computer world's king, the IBM. By having a partnership agreement with the IMB, Bill Gates was able to get IBM to use his operating system in their computers while he got a percentage of the profit.

That was simple, but also powerful enough to make Gates the richest man in the world.

Steve Job was popular for building Apple but he wouldn't have done it so well without the partnership of Steve Wozniak.

You probably might never hear of Google if not for synergy between Larry Page and Sergey Brin.

I've discussed partnership deals with two different people who are experts in what they are doing in the last one month alone.

I live my life as an entrepreneur looking for whose hands to use, who to partner with, who to collaborate with because I know the more good heads I'm able to bring together and the more smart companies I'm able to partner with, the richer I'll be.

If you ask me for how you can become successful faster, I'll tell you to learn how to "cheat" in life's exams.

In school, you were taught to do your exams alone. In life, you must learn how to cheat, how to collaborate, cooperate and partner with other people, businesses and organizations.

That's what this book is all about.

My goal in writing this book is to show you how you can be rich faster, by leveraging on other people's brains, time, resources, energy, etc.

I know if I can get more Africans to understand how to use other people's hands, they will do better with their lives because when two or more people partner together, they bring together their unique strengths, resources and skills. Because of this collaboration, they become more powerful. The more power of synergy and individual or company has, the tougher it is for such individual or company to be defeated by the competition.

That's the reason why you see companies cooperating and collaborating with other companies all the time. That's why you see big companies acquiring many small companies.

It's about synergy. It's about getting other people to cooperate with you, so you'll have more power. It's about looking for people whose skills you lack. It's about using other people's time, energy and skills, so that you'll be stronger than your competition.

Look for people and negotiate with them. Get their skills, talents, resources and energy to work together with you. Don't be a lone ranger in the journey of life or you'll get nowhere. I'll discuss this in details as we move on.

CHAPTER 5

LOOK FOR RICHES BUT IN THE RIGHT WAY

One night in the early 2018 I and my wife were talking about my brother-in-law.

He's a 25 years old hard working guy who thinks he actually doesn't need much money in his life. According to him, he just needs enough money to be comfortable and survive. I mean, he just needs enough money to take care of himself.

Such is a statement from somebody who is not looking for riches

Unfortunately, most people in the world are not actually looking for riches and that is why they do not find it in the first place.

As a matter of law, you cannot find what you are not looking for.

Another side to this law is that you are going to find whatever you look for. And that's why the Bible says: "Knock and the door shall be opened". "Seek and ye shall find".

Jesus Christ said "For whoever asks receives". Such is the law of nature.

It could be a spiritual law; but it is also the law of nature that when we search for something, we'll find it, though it may take time.

Now, if I come out to tell you that most people in the world are not looking for riches, then you would think I'm crazy.

"Why would you tell me people are not looking for riches when everyone talks about money all the time?"

Now I'm here to tell you the truth. Most people are not looking for riches and that is why they cannot find it.

Yes, they wish they could be rich.

Yes, they want to be rich and Yes! They dream they could be rich.

However, they do not really desire riches, and they really do not search or look for riches.

How do you know that people are not actually looking for riches?

Well, there are five basic signs to know people who are not looking for riches.

The first sign to know you're not looking for riches is; **if you are among those people who pretend as if money is not important**, just like my brother-in-law, then, you're not looking for riches (and you can't find it).

If you are among those people would talk or pretend that money is not important when you're in the midst of your friends or your church members, that's the sign that you're not looking for riches.

Why?

Because we can deceive our conscious mind, but we can't deceive our subconscious mind no matter how we pretend. People who talk or think or behave as if money is no important are liars and deceivers to themselves.

Why?

Because you can't become successful or great without money.

Just take a moment and look around you to see whatever you can see all around you now. All these things you see around you or in your environment were bought or built with money.

Without money, you can't really go far in life.

There are so many people in our world who pretend as if money is not important.

They talk about it with nonchalance. They ask: "What is money?"

Religion makes so many people believe this but it's not true. Deep within every human being, he/she knows that money is very important.

Do you know any man who works 12hrs every day and yet says money isn't important?

Do you know any man who hates his job, yet still working, but pretends money isn't that important?

How does that make any sense to anyone?

Why are they working 12hrs every day if money isn't that important?

Why can't they resign in the job they hate, since they believe money isn't that important?

Money can be likened to a lubricant. It partly if not almost oils the wheels of life.
Your marriage depends on money. Taking care of your children depends on money. Making your wife smile most times depends on money. Eating, drinking and living in a good house obviously depends on money.

Even being a true Christian depends so much on money.

I've seen some good Christians doing wrong things because they are poor.

Benjamin Franklin said, **"An empty sack cannot stand"**.

The meaning is, you can't be totally upright if you lack money.

You can't be straightforward all the time if you are poor. It's just as good as an empty sack and empty sack cannot stand.

However, a loaded sack can stand and withstand trials. A hungry man cannot tell the truth all the time and a hungry man cannot be righteous all the time.

Why?

This is because he will always be frustrated. He has to do things he doesn't really like to do.

So, who says money isn't important?

Of course, there are so many other things in life that are far more important than money, things such as your marriage, your kids, your spiritual life, and your social life.

Though they are very important, money makes all of them work.

Now, what am I saying here?

There are so many people in our world who pretend money is not important. And that is one sign that they are not looking for riches. And you can't find riches, if you're not looking for it.

Ultimately, people who aren't looking for riches cannot be rich.

Don't ever say or think money isn't important because you'll be a liar by saying or thinking so.

Yes, life is more than money but money makes every other things work.

The second sign to look for, to know people who cannot be rich because they are not looking for riches is to look for people who believe that they need just little amount of money to take care of themselves.

This is another lie because life is extremely expensive.

Nobody needs "just a little amount" to take care of himself. Anyone who wants to live a normal life needs a lot of money.

The reason is because life is extremely expensive.

Since you have just a life to live, you want to live in a comfortable home, drive a moderate (or nice) car, take very good care of your parents (if you still have them), take good care of your wife, kids, even other people's kids.

If you think "just small money" would be okay for all these, then, you're deceiving yourself.

You know, when people say "If I could get a job that pays me N250, 000 per month, I should be alright", they're not looking for riches.

These people have been deceived to believe that life could be lived with "Just small money".

This isn't true because life is extremely expensive (and becoming more and more expensive day by day).

In the present world, you can't sustain yourself with a little money. You need a whole lot of money. When I say a whole lot of money, I mean a whole lot of money, to live a normal life.

Now, if you're thinking, "If I can get a job of two hundred thousand naira, then I'll be alright. My family and my children would be alright. We will eat, drink, and buy clothes and be fine", then, you're not looking for riches and you shouldn't be reading this book in the first place.

I want you to get me right, I'm not trying to preach covetousness here. I'm just trying to preach abundance. You know abundance is what nature promises us as opposed to scarcity. We have to think about this. If oxygen is abundant, if water is abundant, if natural resources could be abundant; then money could be abundant.

Don't think of having "Just small money". Think of having millions of dollars.

The reason why most people dream of having just a little money is because they think that it's easier to have small money but it's not true.

It's easier to have big money than to have small money.

If you dream of having "Just a little amount", you're going to work for money and worry about money all your life but if you dream of having millions of dollars, you're going to master how to manufacture money by using other people's hands and brains.

People who have little money work all their lives for other people's companies and still retire poor.

People who have a lot of money have great freedom to travel around and work anywhere they want, so why would you want "Just small money"?

I literally don't have an office because I can work anywhere in the world.

I don't wake up with alarm and I don't have hours of work because I can work anytime I want.

I don't have leave because I can stop working anytime I want.

I can travel away from the city I live and do just anything I think is appropriate.

If you think all these is possible for me with "Just #250,000 per month salary", you're joking.

What's my point here?

People who think they don't need much money cannot be wealthy because they are lying. No, they're not really lying but they are not telling the truth.

Tell yourself the truth. The truth is, you need a whole lot of money to live normal life and you need to make such huge amount, legitimately.

Dream Big.

Don't dream of "Just a little amount" or you'll spend the rest of your life working for money.

Dream millions or even billions.

Note; you'll work more if you dream small than if you dream big.

The third sign that shows you are not looking for riches is **when you think that everybody who is rich became rich in a fraudulent way or by luck**.

There's this common belief especially in Africa and the black race generally that when you see someone who is rich or successful, we believe there is a luck or fraud behind such person's wealth or success.

The first time I experienced this was when I became the best student in my school. Some people started thinking that I was a genius. Which of course, I'm not.

They just believed I'm a genius because I do well than all of them in school. Some of them even resorted to calling me a wizard. They thought I was a wizard because I was the most brilliant amongst them all.

What these guys didn't know was that I worked harder than them. For hours, I'd be awake when they were sleeping.

One day I was addressing a group of people and I heard somebody from the crowd saying, "That guy uses 'black power' to talk"

He claimed he knew me and even mentioned the name of my town, just to prove his point.

What is very funny about this story?

While growing up, I fell in love with public speaking. I read a lot of books about human relationship, public speaking, entrepreneurship, leadership and sort of things like that.

Therefore, I tend to use the knowledge I derive from those books in my day to day life. I became a good public speaker and leader.

So, when people discovered I was a good at public speaking, they thought it was the aid of a "black power".

That's how bad many Africans could judge you.

The same way is how they'll judge you when you're rich. Some would say, "He's a thief", others would say, "He did money ritual" while those who love you a little would say, "He's very lucky".

Nor of these people can ever become rich because they have assumed that riches come via fraud, luck or juju.

Well, I'm not here to defend the rich. Instead, I'm here to tell the truth.

As we have business people who are liars and thieves, so do we have lawyers, who are liars and thieves, so do we have teachers who are liars and thieves, so do we have accountants, bankers, secretaries, politicians, and even pastors and Imams who are liars and thieves.

Being honest and being straightforward doesn't have anything to do with your profession or your financial status. It's about your morality. If you look around, you'll see that many successful or wealthy people are far more honest than poor people.

Just as we have honest accountants; so do we have dubious accountants. Just as we have honest entrepreneurs so do we have dubious ones.

What am I saying here?

You are not looking for riches if you believe everyone who is rich becomes rich via fraud, deceit or luck.

When people pretend that money is more important, they are not looking for riches and can never be rich. When people think it is little money they need to be wealthy; well, they can ever become rich because they have actually limited themselves.

When people think being rich is a sin or that everyone who becomes rich does so by lying, deceit or luck, what they're telling themselves is, "I can't be rich because every rich person is a liar, a thief or a fraudster".

Being wealthy is an honourable thing and should be desired by everyone.

So many people have become extremely wealthy without cheating anyone or lying to anyone and it's hardly by luck. You have to desire wealth and follow the principles that will make you wealthy, as discussed inside this book.

Don't think the rich are liars. Don't think they are cheating the poor. Don't believe they are lucky.

If you think or believe any of the above, you're deceiving yourself and you may die poor.

The fourth sign that shows that you are not looking for riches is **when you are not looking for opportunities or discussing opportunities among your friends**.

I find myself fortunate because I grew up among passionate friends.

I remember as far back as when I was a young guy of about 18/19, I was broke, I didn't have a penny in my bank account; yet, I would gather in the room with my friends and we could discuss business ideas for thirty minutes to five hours.

Just discussing those ideas always got me excited. Sometimes, we'd discuss about business all night.

I mean, these were young and broke guys. These were guys who didn't even have five dollars in their bank accounts. Yet, we were always talking about business ideas.

I remember talking to one of my friends about a business idea and we thought of buying some filling stations that weren't functioning any longer.

We were planning how we could buy and resell those filling stations, even when we didn't have any money.

That was how I grew up. And as I grew up, I was always looking for opportunities.

Now, the fourth sign that shows you are not looking for riches and that you can never be rich is if you are not looking for the business opportunities in your country.

If you just wake up in the morning, take your bath, put on your clothes and run to work, come back from work and sleep, or argue about football, hockey, politics, or whatever, then you're not looking for riches.

If you are not looking for or thinking about opportunities in your country, if you are not discussing business ideas with your friends, if you are not meeting people who really matters, who discuss business ideas, who discuss opportunities, you are not looking for riches and you can never be rich.

A friend of mine told me about some guys he met around 5:30 am in the morning. These guys were discussing football.

So many people discuss politics, football, gossips etc., in the public transport, at their working place and just every other place but they never discuss opportunities.

Tell me what you're discussing and I'll tell you what you're thinking all day long. Tell me what you're thinking about all day long and I'll tell you your future.

The truth is, most people don't like to be rich (but they won't believe that's true).

What you want to be is what you think about all day. What you think about is what you'll discuss.

I don't discuss football because I don't think about it. I don't discuss what's happening in Hollywood because I don't think about their gossip. I rarely discuss politics because I rarely think about it.

I think about business and Jesus and those are the two topics you'll hear me discuss, nine out of ten times.

If you don't look for, think about or discuss opportunities in your country, or you even believe they aren't available, then, you can't be rich.

It doesn't matter whether you have money now or you don't. Look for the opportunities to create wealth, don't make friends with people who don't discuss great ideas, focus your mind on how you can build wealth, not on what the politicians or entertainers are doing.

The fifth and last sign that shows you are not looking for riches and that you may never ever become rich is if you are not reading about money or business.

There are people who wake up in the morning and hurry up to the newspaper stand or visit a website to read about Chelsea, Liverpool, Barcelona, and Arsenal.

These guys read about sports or other trending topics every single day of their life.

There are people who wake up in the morning to read or watch political news and want to know what the president of countries have said or done. They do this every day of their lives.

There are people who wake up in the morning to read about gossips in Hollywood or Nollywood and they have websites where they do that and they do this every single day of their life.

There are people who read pornographic materials or watch pornographic films.
You would be surprised to know that pornography websites are one of the most popular websites and most visited websites all over the world, even though people don't talk about pornography.

Think about it for a moment. Your co-workers don't talk about pornography. Your friends don't talk about pornography.

Your wife doesn't talk about phonograph. Nobody is talking about it yet most people consume pornographic materials because people always have time to think and to read and watch videos about things they care about.

Tell me everything you've read, listened to and watched in the last 7 days and I'll tell you your future.

Most times Africans blame God or Satan for whatever happens to them (either poverty or disease). While I believe in Jesus and I know Satan exists, I think we are mostly to be blamed for our woes in Africa.

You are what you read, listen to and watch.

If you want to know how your future would look like, simply make a list of everything you've read, listened to and watched in the last 7 days.

If you spend all your time reading about sport, you'll become a sport spectator. If you read and listen to every political happenings, you may become a poor political "scientist".

How can you ever hope to become rich when you don't read about money and business every day?

I don't watch or read about sport. I don't watch or discuss about movies. But I've read, listened to audios or watched videos about money or business almost every day of my last 12 years.

You're what you read, watch or listen to.

You want to change your life?

Change what you read, listen to and watch.

Everyone read, listen to and watch videos about what they love.

The fact that you're not reading about money is an indication that you don't want to be rich.

The fact that you don't listen to the audio tapes or watch videos about business and money is an indication that you hate being wealthy.

Don't argue with me because I'm telling you the truth.

Yes, I know you want to be rich. I know you wish to be rich.

But I'm saying you don't desire to be rich.

People can want anything and they won't do anything about it. People can wish anything and they won't do anything about it. But it's not possible to desire something and not do anything about it.

So many people want to lose weight but do nothing to lose weight. So many people wish to stop smoking and still continue smoking.

You can wish or want to be rich and still get busy reading about gossips, soccer and politics. However, if you desire to be rich, you'll think about it all day, search Google to learn anything related to being rich, visit YouTube to watch videos of business people, buy books about money and business (Thank God you bought and read this book).

Go through all these 5 signs and see which of them you really need to work on.

1. Don't say or think you need just small amount of money. Tell yourself that you need millions of dollars and start dreaming it.
2. Don't say or think money isn't that important. Confess that money makes everything in the world works and you need so much of it.
3. Don't ever believe that the rich are thieves, liars or lucky or you'll not strive to be rich.
4. Don't make friends with people who only discuss football, politics and gossips. Look for and discuss business opportunities and how to build wealth.
5. Don't read just entertainment, political and soccer news. Read about money. Listen to audio tapes about business. Watch videos about success

Look for riches. It's a Godly and righteous thing to do.

CONCLUSION TO SECTION 2

The first section of this book is to show you that the ONLY way you can ever become rich and successful is by using other people's brains, time, energy and resources. In other words, you need to "cheat" if you want to pass life's exams. Unlike school's exams, you need to ask for help and depend on the other people's skills, knowledge and resources. You need to partner, collaborate, employ and form synergy with other people.

You wish to go alone? You'll get nowhere.

The second section of this book was designed to show the means to the end. I wanted to show you how to discover great ideas that will allow you to build empires, which will allow you to be able to use other people's time, brains and energy.

Chapter one of the second section teaches that you should look for change. Chapter two teaches that you should look for problems. Chapter three teaches that you should look for knowledge. Chapter four teaches that you should look for people.
Chapter five teaches that you should look for riches.

If you actively look for all these five "powers", you'll have the strong foundation upon which to build your empire which will help you to use other people's time and energy to be rich.

The third section of this book will be about what you shouldn't look for, if you truly want to be rich.

Let's get started!

SECTION THREE
WHAT NOT TO LOOK AT, IF YOU WANT TO BE RICH

CHAPTER 1
STOP LOOKING AT THE REAR-VIEW MIRROR

A couple of weeks ago, I received a call from a man who said he had problems. According to him, he was unable to complete school because he didn't have anyone to help him as a young boy.

The man went on and on complaining about how he became so poor as a result of not completing his "education" (which to me is just schooling, NOT education).

That's a typical example of people who keep on looking at the rear-view mirrors.

Rear-view mirrors are designed for drivers to look at the back and know what's happening behind once in a while. For instance, let's say you're driving from Lagos to Abuja. You have to check your rearview mirror occasionally through your entire journey.

The rear-view mirror was not designed for you to look at constantly. It was designed to be used occasionally by the driver.

Back to the man who constantly thought about his past.

Dwelling constantly on your past won't solve your problems. It would only worsen it; as you'll never be able to rise above constant complaint about your past.

Your past is like a rear-view mirror.

Just imagine a driver driving and consistently looking at the rear-view mirror. What do you think would happen?

Accident, of course!

And that's how some drivers get involved in accidents because they constantly look at their rear-view mirrors.

When you keep on looking at your rear-view mirror, you'll always complain.

You'll keep on thinking: "Oh! My life wouldn't have turned out so if my parents weren't poor". "My life wouldn't have turned out so if my father was able to send me to school". "My life wouldn't have turned out so if I wasn't born in Africa".

So many people in Africa look at the rear-view mirror, complaining every day about what was wrong with their background, country and continent and that's the reason they remain poor.

Your life is like a car and your background is the rear-view mirror you should look at once in a while. Constantly looking at the back won't change anything__ you'd most likely end up having an accident (poverty).

As a driver, you will not drive home safely (become great or successful) if you keep looking at the rear-view mirror (background).

If you keep on looking at your background, you will never become successful.

Why?
Because you'll always have reasons to make excuses!

Listen, **everyone has a pathetic story to tell.**

Everyone has something that is not good about their background.

People who become successful simply stopped thinking about their background.

They stopped looking at their rear-view mirror. Instead, they focused on how to make their lives great.

Bill Clinton was born on August 19, 1946, few months after his father died so Clinton never saw his dad.

His mother moved him from one man to the other; many of whom usually treated his mother badly.

As Clinton grew, he had two options. He could tell himself, "I have no father to take care of me" but he told himself, "Well, my father died at 29. And since I could die at 29 too, I have to be in a hurry". So, Bill Clinton took his life very seriously, remained focus and read ferociously. Within certain two years, Bill Clinton read over 300 books.

Why? Because he wanted to achieve things fast because he knew he could die at 29 too.

Years later, Clinton became a lecturer of law in the university; an Attorney General at 29; a governor at 32 and president of the United States at 47.

Now, this is a guy who had a very rough background and knew that if he kept worrying about his background, he'd never become successful.

Stop making excuses about your background. Focus on the future.

Thomas Edison was taken away from school because they thought he was unintelligent. That was horrible!

Just imagine being withdrawn from the school because you're considered dumb!

While it was painful, Thomas knew he had to stop dwelling on the past if he wanted to become successful in life.

Thomas Edison went on to become the greatest inventor of the 20th Century.
Until you forget your background, your back will be on the ground.

Some people would say, "But Steve, all these men are from the United States and they have better opportunities".

Well, that's how most Africans make excuses. They believe that the reason some people succeed is because they live in 'better' countries, forgetting that, even in the so call 'better' countries, 90% of people end up as failures.

If people become rich because of the countries they reside in, why are many people in the United Kingdom and United States of America still poor?

If you're one of those who think, "But, these guys live in better country", I'll share Africans stories with you.

Mike Adenuga was born by a teacher.

As a young boy, Adenuga often hawked goat feed in the streets of Ibadan. While growing up, things were tough for his family, but the young boy decided to change his life.

He could only do this by forgetting the past and focusing on the future. The young Adenuga could have complained about everything, from the bad economy to bad government and poor parents, but that would have kept him a poor man

Adenuga had to become a driver and a security guard, as some of those things he had to do to rise up.

At 26, he had started doing well with his life.

Today, Mike Adenuga is a billionaire and one of the richest Africans.

Stop troubling yourself about what you don't have control over. You can't change who gave birth to you, your country of birth neither can you return to when you were age 10 to attend better school.

In fact, you can't control the economy or make the political leaders do well.

All these are your backgrounds. You must leave them behind and focus on your future.
Seek knowledge; focus on looking for opportunities, changes, problems you can solve, etc.

You have a very terrible background?

And so what!

I'm telling stories about these people so you'll realise they were all nobody before they became somebody. How did they do it?

They never focused on their past. They focused on how to become successful.

There's a book called Millionaire's Next Door. The authors of the book discovered that 85% of millionaires in the America were self-made, they were people who weren't born rich but they decided to become successful and for them to become wealthy, they had to forget their backgrounds.

Why?

Because you can't drive forward while you are looking backward!

It's just like you can't walk on the street and continue looking backwards. If you want to move forward, you can't keep looking at the rear-view mirror.

All the successful men I have mentioned had to forget their backgrounds and focus on what they wanted to achieve (success and financial prosperity).

But wait!

I've been telling you stories about people who have become successful. You'd probably doubt the accuracy of the story since they aren't personal stories.

Therefore, I'd like to tell you my own personal story.

Like most people in Africa, I was born into a very poor family. My family was very happy that they'd given birth to a baby boy (because in Africa, giving birth to a boy is a thing of joy).

However, this joy didn't last long. After a few months, my parents discovered that I was sickly.
That's where my mother's struggles started. I often become sick twice every month. It was rheumatism and so terrible that I would cry all day and night.

I'd beg God to kill me because the pain got worse with every occurrence. I would feel the pain all over my body.

I could go to bed as a normal person, only to wake up hours later in pains. I found it difficult to lift my hands or legs. This condition would last for between five days and a week.

I'd recover and enjoy good health for a week or two, only to relapse.

As a result, the first 15-17 years of my life was a horrible experience. Now, what made it even worse was that my parents never took me to a hospital to check what was wrong with me.

This was probably because we lived in a village. For the first 14 years of my life, I was never taken to a hospital to undergo a test for what was wrong with my health.

You can imagine being down with ulcer or typhoid yet being administered malaria medications.

As at that time, my parents were actually using wrong medications for me. My mother (a one-in-a-million) even took me to prophets and herbalists, just to get a cure.

That was what she knew she could, as an African.

She didn't know it could be a medical condition. She attributed it to the handiwork of 'witches'.

Since my village lacked so many social amenities, I couldn't read or speak good English like city kids.

There was no electricity. I couldn't even remember seeing a television in the entire village. There were neither good access roads nor portable water; all we had was a stream.

And since my father was a cocoa farmer, we grew up on the farm. We had to go to the farm every time we were free from school.

Of course, we had a primary school, but no secondary school in the entire village.
In other words, I was born in a poverty-stricken village, to uneducated parents, in a bad health. However, when I clocked 18 years, I told myself that I am responsible for my future regardless of my background.

I started dreaming of becoming famous, rich and successful. I stopped wasting time on football, movie and gossips and started reading books about success and achievement.

The more I learned from successful people, the more I desired to become like them.

You might have read other parts of my stories somewhere else. Today, I'm famous, achieved some levels of success and have more money to throw around than most people.

Till today, most people who grew up in my village are poor and angry. They think their poverty is as a result of their background but it's because they fixed their gaze on their background.

I've got here because of the grace of God, the grace that taught me how to focus on the future, not my ugly background.

It doesn't matter if your background isn't or is as worse as mine!

What matters is that you are willing to take responsibility and focus on your future, not your yesterday or today.

Your background was in the past. Your future is in your hands.

Back to the caller who made excuses to be happy. I asked him: "You are telling me you don't have education, but you are speaking good English; what else do you call education?"

You are telling me you're living in poverty. You're telling me your father didn't have enough money to make you complete your "education".

All those excuses don't make any sense.

What would you tell your children?

Would you tell your son that the reason you cannot give him a good life is because your father didn't take care of you?
Would you tell your daughter that the reason you're poor is because your father was poor?

Do you have any excuse for not taking care of your wife?

Bury these excuses; nobody cares!

Your children deserve a good life and it's your responsibility to make it happen.

Your wife deserves a good life and excuses will not give her such.

If you're a woman, your children deserve a great life and they don't want to listen to your boring stories of how you were born poor.

Yesterday was an accident (because we didn't plan it) and tomorrow is our design (because we are the architect).

We had no control over our background but we can design our future.

We would never progress if we keep being busy about what our parents didn't do for us, or what our family didn't do, or what our political leaders didn't do.

What have you done for yourself?

Most often than not when we talk about what people didn't do for us, we forget to talk about what we didn't do for ourselves.

When we talk about how governments hurt us, we are often quiet about how we kill ourselves.

When you tell me your parents didn't send you to school, what steps (as an adult) have you taken to educate yourself?

If you weren't enrolled into school, now that you're 25 years, pick up good books; read them and educate yourself.

Stop blaming your parents; stop blaming your father who was poor and couldn't cater for you; stop telling yourself you're stuck.

As an adult, make use of your energy and brain for the right things.
You keep on blaming your father for what he didn't do. Yet, you don't blame yourself for what you don't do.

That is what I call irresponsibility.

You've left school for more than five years and you've not read even 10 books about money or how to improve your financial situation.

The last time you tried to start a business, you retreated immediately after the first failure.

You wake up every day to think about what's bad in your country, not what you can make good.

Truly, government may be hurting you, but you're surely killing yourself.

How does that make sense to me if you talk about what government does to make you poor but you don't talk about what you're doing to make yourself wretched?

Do you blame yourself when you wake up each day to social media and sleep every night on gossip sites? Do you point finger at yourself for having two, three social media accounts? Do you blame yourself for wasting ten hours every week in front of the TV?

Do you blame yourself for being a pessimist? Do you blame yourself for wasting time? Do you blame yourself for being a coward who cannot endure business failures? Do you blame yourself for not reading good books?

If you don't blame yourself for not doing what you should do to make your life better, how can you blame the government that careless if you exist?

You'll be justified for blaming your father for your poverty, if you blame yourself first.

You'll be right to point one finger to your background, if you point the remaining four to yourself.

If you're poor today as an African, I'll agree with you that your background contributed to your poverty, but guess what? It's 70/30.

Your decisions, indecisions and habits are responsible for the 70% of the reason(s) you're poor while your background is responsible for the 30%. Until you see it this way, you won't change your life.
If it's going to be, it's up to you.

Stop fixing your gaze on your background. Stop looking at the rear-view mirror.

Take responsibility for your life and focus on the future you desire.

Forget the yesterday and focus on building your great tomorrow.

This is the mind-set that can help you to become a rich person.

CHAPTER 2
STOP LOOKING AT THE SIDE MIRROR

In the previous chapter of this book, I explained to you that you really have to stop looking at the rear-view mirror.

I explained that the rear-view mirror is meant for drivers to see the back. I also explained that when you keep looking at your rear-view mirror, you won't be able to drive properly; which can lead to something disastrous such as an accident.

What I explained in the previous chapter means that you should stop looking constantly or complaining about your parents, country or continent.

You have to forget the ugliness in your background because if you keep on using them as excuses, if you keep murmuring and worrying about your background, it would drag your back to the ground.

Now, in this chapter, you are going to learn not to look at your side mirror.

Side mirror is meant for a driver to see what's coming on his side. While it's good (once in a while) to look at the side mirror, any driver who fixes his gaze on the side mirror will either not drive fast or crash.

Every day, when I listen to or meet people, what I hear them talk about most of the time is how bad the governments of their counties are.

You'd hear them lament: "Oh! This country doesn't have electricity as a result of bad governance". "We don't have good roads in our country because we have bad government"

"All our political leaders are thieves, and that is why we are poor". "I'm unemployed because the Nigerian government cannot give me a job"

"I'm poor today because the government is responsible for the economic situation that made my company sack me".

That's what you'll hear people say when you go around.

Such people keep blaming the government for everything.

That is what I call 'looking at the side mirror'.

Am I trying to make it look as if the government is good? Definitely not!

Am I trying to criticize people who criticize government by telling them that they are wrong? Not at all!

It's only that, from experience, I know and understand that you can never achieve anything with your life as long as you concentrate on what the government is doing or not doing.

Maybe I should resort to history, to the time of our forefathers. During those years, they spent all their days complaining about the government.

A couple of months ago, I listened to some evergreen songs by Sunny Ade, Nigeria's musical maestro.

As I did, I noticed the lyrics involved soliciting the government. He said: "Government!
Please help us. *Garri* is expensive…Rice's expensive…Oil is expensive, etc."

Funny enough, this was a song that was written about 40 years ago.

Now, can you imagine; even 40 years ago, somebody was complaining that rice was expensive? That *Garri* was expensive?

So what about now? What about today?
If rice was expensive in the 70s and people complained, what should the people of today do?

The thing is: people have always complained about the government.

Now, remember I told you that I'm not trying to defend the government here. I'm only trying to tell you that complaint is a distraction.

As long as you keep looking at the side mirror, you'll get distracted. You can't fix gaze eye at the side mirror and drive fast!

So, as long as you keep on complaining and paying attention to what the government does right, or what they don't do right; you can't pay attention to your own life because you'll be irresponsible.

You'll say to yourself, "I'm poor because the government is bad".

That's irresponsibility!

When Africans complain that the reason they are unemployed or poor is because government is bad, they're saying two things to themselves.

First, they're saying that the reason they're poor is because the government is bad and that they can never become rich until the government becomes good.

Few days ago I read a comment from a man who wrote "Until there's stable power supply, you can't build successful business in Nigeria"

Little did he know that many of his age mates are already building great companies in Nigeria, even with poor power supply.

To expect a 'good' government before you'll be rich is to expect green vegetables in the desert. It's possible, but only with miracle.

Forget the government; it may never be 'good'!

Complaining about what the government has failed to do is a big distraction to your mind.

You can't build substantial wealth until you can concentrate your entire mind's power on a single goal (without any distraction).

You need to concentrate all your energy, resources, and time on building wealth. People who constantly complain about the government can't concentrate on their lives because they are always angry.

You know why they are always angry? It's because such people have too many things to be angry about.

I'm writing these words with a personal computer powered by an electricity generating set because electricity in my country is still very bad, even in 2018. That alone is enough to make you angry all day.

Each time you go out in most towns in Africa, you'll see bad roads. That alone is enough to make you complain for three hours.

Just visit an African news blog now and you'll read about how someone has stolen billions. That alone is enough to spoil your day.

Now you see the problem. You can't focus on your life at the same time when you focus on the government's failures because there are too many of them.

Focusing on what government is doing mean you'll spend your days angry, sad and complaining. How can you be productive with such destructive emotions?

You care about success?

Focus (solely) on how to achieve it.

I know you need government, but not as much as you think.

You actually need yourself much more than you need any government.

Stop looking at the side mirror because it's a distraction.

CHAPTER 3
STOP LOOKING AT THE SUN! YOU DON'T HAVE POWER OVER IT.

So it happens that when family members call me, they often ask how I cope with the economic situation.

These people believe that your life depends on the economy of your country, so if the economy of your country is bad, you're likely to be poor.

So many people believe that the reason they're poor is because the economy is bad.

Let me make these two points very clear.

The first is that economy being good or bad is a natural thing. For instance, if you're 70 years, you must have witnessed one major and one minor economic crisis because every human being who will live up to 65 years is likely to go through two economic crises.

This is to tell you that a bad economy is not a mystery, it's not something unusual. It's something the world experiences every now and then.

It's just like the Sun. You may not like the Sun when it's hot, but you don't have any control over it.

You may not like the economy when it's bad, but you have no control over it.

Great people focus on what they can control while ordinary people focus on what is beyond them.

As a matter of law, if you want to be successful in life, you'll stop focusing on things you don't have control over, one of which is the economy.

It doesn't matter who you are, you can't control the Sun, so why waste time crying because it's hot?

The right thing to do could be to get an umbrella and that's what most people don't do.

The only thing you can do when the economy is bad is to focus on how to become more creative in helping other humans solve their problems with products or services.

Complaining about a bad economy is as good as complaining about a hot Sun. It's a pure waste of your precious time.

While so many people believe that when the economy is bad they can't succeed, people who decide not to complain about the Sun look for an umbrella.

That's the reason you'll see certain people becoming richer, even when the economy is bad.

In fact, many of today's multinational corporations started when the economy was bad.

The likes of General Electric (1890), IBM, (1896), Disney (1923), Burger King (1953), CNN (1980) and Microsoft (1980) all began at a time of economic crisis in their respective countries.

I went fully into the business world in 2008, when the entire world's economy was experiencing a meltdown.

What's my point here?

At that time when you hear people say, "The economy is bad", some other people somewhere said, "We can build a company, using the opportunity of this economic situation."

It's all about what you decide to believe.

In the previous chapter, I explained that in every change there's an opportunity. Now, that actually means that about the time one person says economy is bad, another had become rich or richer.

Why?

This is because the economy being bad is a 'change'. And like I mentioned earlier, every 'change'; whether good or bad, is like a moment of opportunity for people who look for business opportunities.

So, when you hear in the news that the economy of your country is bad, you can be sure that someone is making some real cash.

Stop looking at the Sun; you have no power over it. Go buy an umbrella instead.
Stop looking at your country's economy.

You have no power over it.

It's irresponsible people who focus their life and attention on what they don't have control over.

Great people focus on what they can change and work so hard to change what they can.

Whether the economy is going to be better or worse next week, can you do anything about it?

Why worry or focus on things you cannot change?

Let it be!

Let your country's economy be!

Focus on what you can control – your personal economy.

The fact that your country's economy is bad doesn't mean that you have to be poor. In fact, it could be an opportunity for you to be wealthy as I've explained earlier. The fact that your country's economy is good or stable doesn't mean you're going to be wealthy.

In fact, your country's economic status isn't a variable that should be used to determine your potential to be wealthy or otherwise.

Your wealth is in your mind!

Yes, I agree that building a business during an economic crisis could be tough, just as walking in the scorching sun could be tough. But since there's nothing you can do about it, it is better you don't focus on it.

Focus on getting an umbrella, not on the hot sun. Focus on looking for business opportunities, not on bad economy.

You get what you look for. You are attracted to what you focus on.

Let me conclude this chapter with an illustration about a ship.

When you see a ship at sea, you'd think this is dangerous. However, as long as the water doesn't enter the ship to a point where it is overwhelmed the ship is safe.
The ship can travel thousands of miles to its destination without an issue.

So, no matter what goes on around you, you'll stay afloat for as long as you don't allow yourself to be overwhelmed.

We both know that, in comparison, the size of a ship or boat to that of the sea can be likened to a small seed floating on water. In spite of that, the ship remains afloat.

Of course, there could be turbulent water and the ship could sway sideways, but until the water finds its way into the ship, the ship or boat is safe.

So, until what is happening around get inside you, nothing much has happened.

Yes, the economy of your country could be bad as a result of inflation, unemployment or any other crisis or you could be encountering a rough time; you'll end up rich as long as you keep a diligent watch over your mind, thought and belief.

Stop looking at the Sun. You have no control over it. Get an umbrella instead.

CHAPTER 4
STOP LOOKING AT THE UNITED KINGDOM OR UNITED STATES

Now, if you are the type that keeps a tab on the global happenings, you probably would have read about how numerous young Africans struggle to migrate to "better" countries.

Most borrow money from friends, families, and even strangers. A few others even go as far as selling their father's properties.

While some travel by air, others take riskier routes travelling through the desert and the Mediterranean Sea.

Why do they go through all these?

They are desperate to leave Africa because they believe that there's wealth and success in the United States of America, United Kingdom, Europe etc.

Now, I have reasons to believe these people don't believe in themselves. They don't believe they can make it in their countries.

On a certain day, while in my late teens, my step-brother came to me and gave me a form to fill. It happened to be a visa lottery form.

During those years there was mad rush to fill visa lottery forms. In fact, about two or three family members of mine migrated to the United States of America through the program.

I could have travelled as teenager but I thought something was wrong with leaving my country for monetary reasons.

The question I asked myself was: "Why must I leave my country because of money?" Somehow, I understood that money and problems are related.

Most often than not, wherever you see money, you'd find problems lurking around. And whenever you see problem, you can be sure money is involved along that axis.

I discovered that my country (Nigeria) had a lot problems compared to the United States of America or the United Kingdom.

If problems and money are inseparable, why should I run to a country that doesn't have many problems since I want to become wealthy?

That is my mind-set!

Even when I was a young boy and had no *kobo*, I believed that I shouldn't leave my country because of money.

Now listen; there is nothing bad about travelling around the world. You can visit the United Kingdom, United States of America, Europe, Asia, or wherever you intend but you should go to these countries for the right reasons.

You shouldn't leave your country because you want to make money. It's one of the silliest mistakes you could ever make in your life.

The reason is because money is not a product of a country or a location, but a product of mind.

As long as your mind is poor, you are going to be poor. Where you live doesn't matter; if your mind is rich, you are going to be rich.

There was a time in my life when my wife and I were living in our small town.

Interestingly, I was making more money in that town than almost everyone else. In fact, I was making more money from this little town, than most people in Lagos, Abuja, and Port Harcourt – regarded the cities 'richest' in Nigeria.

How was that possible?

Well, that happened because I understood that wealth creation does not have anything to do with your physical location. It's all about your mind.

If you like, you can travel to the richest countries of the world, as long as you don't change your mind set about money, you'll only get 'good job', pay higher bills, higher taxes and return broke to your country of origin.

Don't look for money in the United States of America or any other foreign country, because money isn't there!

Stop dreaming of fleeing from Africa, instead, start looking for the opportunities in Africa.
Interestingly, what most people don't know is that it's easier to get rich in Africa than in many other parts of the world.

The reason is very simple. Problems and money are brothers. Wherever you see more problems, be sure more money is there because people only become rich by solving problems.

I have a friend who borrowed all the money he could get, and sold any property he had in order to run away from Nigeria to Canada.

Today I'm richer than him and there are millions of them like that.

When African leaders have problems in their countries, they look up to the developed countries such as China, America and Britain for help, just as when Africans have problem, they look up to their leaders.

This dependence mentality is what is killing us, and we have to stop it.

Either as countries or as individuals, we don't need help from the United Kingdom or the United States of America. As long as Africans believe that they need help from such countries, the continent or its people will never become prosperous.

Start believing in Africa; stop regarding yourself a victim in Africa; start referring to yourself as a solution to the problems of Africa.

Stop dreaming of going to the United Kingdom or United States of America in search for money via employment.

Stop looking up to United Kingdom or United States of America. Instead, look at Africa and look at yourself; change your mind so that you'll be able to solve some problems and make a change in Africa.

That's how to be wealthy.

CHAPTER 5
STOP LOOKING AT POVERTY

Most people lack one basic understanding – the more you do something, the more you get attracted to that thing.

The more you think about something, the more you're attracted to that thing.

The more your mind processes something, the higher your chance of having it.

Now, if you look at our culture, you will understand that so many people spend their entire lives worrying about poverty.

That's the easiest way to be poor.

There is a difference between worrying about poverty and pursuing riches.

People who worry about poverty wake up in the morning and worry about how their kids are growing up, and how to get money to send them to the university.

"How on earth am I going to able to take good care of these three children when everything is now becoming expensive?"

People who worry about poverty can't sleep properly at night. They'd go to bed complaining about the country's economy, about their salary which isn't enough to take care of them, talk less of their family.

They ask: "What would happen in the next five years?"

These thoughts are the complete opposite of the thoughts people who pursue riches entertain.

Even if they have no penny in their bank account, people who pursue riches wake up in the morning and tell themselves "Oh! My kids are growing so fast. My current income isn't enough to sustain us. How can I double our income before next year when my first son would be admitted into the university?"

If you look at the two scenarios, you'd realise that these two categories of people have different ways of thinking. While the first person worries about the high cost of items in the country, the second person thinks about how to improve his financial status to enable him afford things that are becoming more expensive.

While the first person worries about the fact that he might not be able to withstand the financial costs of giving his kids good life, the second person is thinking about how he would double his income.

For instance, while the first man will worry that he may never drive a new car because of increasing cost of automobile; the second person would think about how to triple his income in order to afford a new car in the year after.

While the first man is looking for poverty, the second man is looking for riches.

Most people in our society are looking for poverty. It's only very few people that are looking for riches.

In your heart, you'd assume that it's not possible that you'll be looking for poverty, yet, when you worry about poverty, you're simply looking for poverty.

Don't worry about poverty; think about riches.

Don't say, "Things are expensive", instead, ask yourself, "How can I make enough money to afford anything I want?"

Don't yell at your children, "I don't have money!" Gently tell them, "I'll soon have enough money to get you whatever you want".

Don't live with the idea that money is scarce because it's a lie. Money isn't scarce! Humans simply love to think, talk and look for poverty.

Think, talk and look for wealth and you'll find more than enough of it because you'll always be attracted to whatever you think and talk about.

Whatever you look for is what you'll get.

I usually tell my close friends (even when I had no money), "You see, if God doesn't kill me, the least I can become is a millionaire"

If you truly want to become wealthy, you have to decide in your mind that poverty is not for you. When you believe that poverty isn't for you, you won't think about poverty even if you don't have money at the moment. You'll instead concentrate on creating wealth.

It's like when you're waiting on the road for a red car, the only car you want to see is a red car and that's what your mind looks for. A black car might drive pass you, a green car might even stop in front of you, but you won't pay attention to them for as long as they're not red.

You may be broke and have no money, as long as you've convinced yourself that you can never be poor, you'll concentrate on how to create wealth.

If you hate poverty, don't think poverty. If you love abundance, think and talk abundance.

I love to talk to my friends about how I'll build a ₦50 million house. I love to think about how I'll start two charity organisations. I love to think and talk about how I'll travel all around the world.

Whenever I hear my wife say, "That thing is expensive", I'll tell her, "No. It's not"

Stop looking for poverty. Stop believing you can ever be poor.

Convince yourself that poverty is real, but not for you.

SECTION THREE'S CONCLUSION

If you eat good meals, you're going to be healthy. But that's if you don't eat bad meals together with good meals.

While eating fruits and vegetables can make you healthier, smoking, excessive sugar and alcohol could make your health worse, even when you eat vegetables and fruits.

While section two of this book was written to show you what you must look for (change, problems, knowledge, people and riches), the section three was written to show you what you should not look for, if you want to be rich.

SECTION FOUR
THE HANDS TO USE

If there's one single thing I want to achieve with this book, it's to inspire Africans to learn how to "cheat" in the life's exams.

I want you to be on the lookout for the opportunity to use what you don't have because nobody can ever become rich or successful by his/her own power. Those who go far in life are those who learn and master how to use other people's brains, time, energy, resources, etc. legitimately.

Ordinarily if you ask me; "Whose brains and hands should I use to become successful?", I'll answer you; "Every brains and hands you can legitimately find". However in this section, I'm going to discuss five major "hands" and "brains" you need to actively use.

CHAPTER 1
USE THE HANDS OF YOUR FRIENDS

In the year 2015 there are about, just after a busy day, I called one of my friends whose name is Ikenna "Hello friend, how are you doing?"

As we started talking, because he's an entrepreneur like myself, we started talking about business and few other things.

I was asking him some questions and telling him few things about my business.

"I have studied to know that people who do it in the other way could get better result", he said about what I told him I was doing.

I went to bed that night with a better idea

The next morning I started working on the new idea I got from my friend and before you know it, that idea alone increased my business' profit by almost 200%.

That is the power of friendship but that's not big enough.

In the year 2017, we launched one of our companies and as we were planning our marketing strategies and the launch, I was on phone with one of my friends who knows so much about technology trends.

My initial plan was to get him to work on some technical parts of the company's set up, but it ended up being greater than that.

My friend told me, "We're going to run our marketing campaigns using bot"

That was the first time I heard that there's anything call "bot" so I needed to ask few more questions, search the internet to study what bot is and how it works.

With his guidance, we set up the bot and got it running for our marketing campaign within two weeks.

Can you guess how much that information worth to our business?

I would say more than 5 million Naira.

Now, why do I tell you these stories?

I told you these personal stories to show you the power of friendship.

One day in 2008, I just lost my business and was trying to get myself feet back to the business world. I called one of my friends and asked him for help. While this man was going to the bank, he was delayed by the usual Lagos traffic congestion. Because he never wanted the bank to be closed before he got to the bank, he had to jump on a bike and run to the bank to send me money.

I once spoke to a friend about my business plan. Few days after, he gave me the money he ought not to give me ___ his school fee.

I have tens of stories to tell you about how friends have been so helpful in my journey of life.

It's not just about me. Everyone who has become successful has always been "people's person".

If you want to go far in life, you must build network of great friends around yourself.

If you fail to have friends or walk with average people, you're never going to go far in life.

Make friends with positive people and use their hands.

Just as I emphasize all through this book, using your friends' hands is a good thing to do.

I love my friends and serve them. It brings me joy when they use my hands, just because we're friends.

I surround myself with a lot of good people, yes, because I know I need them for inspiration and challenge. But I'll always look for ways to contribute to their lives, first. Please, do the same.

Yes, the quality of your friends determines the quality of your life, but you don't want to make friends because you want to use them.

You want to make good friends, share whatever you have with them, love them and keep your friendship active with them.

Many at times, the most precious gifts your friends will give you will not be money. Think about a friend whose advice doubled the income of my business and a friend whose knowledge worth five million Naira to our business. All these and many favour I've received from friends in the last decade are not monetary yet, they are priceless.

Some of my friends have done me a great favour by borrowing me books. While these books changed my life, without my friends, I might never get to know those books.

Yes, I have many friends who have helped me with their money, but that's not the primary thing.

The inspiration, ideas, knowledge, insights I get from my friends worth millions to me.

If you desire to go far in life, you can't possibly go alone or go with negative, ordinary people.

You want to surround yourself with positive people who want to do something great with their lives.

The more of such people you have around you, the more successful you can be.

How Can You Get Started.

First, be conscious of people you spend time with.

If you spend time with negative people, you'll end up becoming negative. You can love everyone but you shouldn't be friends with everyone.

The second important thing is, be a people person.

Whether you're in a public transport, in a meeting or in a church, whenever you notice anyone who is positive and seems to be going somewhere in life, connect with them as soon as you can.

Don't sound as if you need them. Just greet, appreciate one or two things about them and exchange contacts with them.

Don't be like most people who believe that their Facebook friends are their friends. It's a lie.

Your friends are people you talk on phone regularly, meet in the physical world if you're in the same city and share real life experience as much as possible.

One of the most valuable assets you can ever have is your friendship because you can use the hands, energy and resources of your friends to become rich faster.

Did I ever told you the story of how a friends invested three million Naira into my business, even though he didn't know anybody in my family and he didn't ask for collateral?

One of the cheapest brains you can use to become rich are your friends' brains but you need to consciously make friends that matter.

If you don't care about the quality of the people you spend time with, you don't care about success.

Build a tall wall of great friends around yourself and keep that friendship active.

This can make you succeed faster than most things on Earth.

CHAPTER 2
USE THE TIME & ENERGY OF YOUR PARTNERS

To go far in life, you must be a "networker".

One of most important things you can do with your life is to network with people, both on a friendship level and on business level.

The whole idea of this book is to challenge you to stop being "self-confident", to stop believing in your ability to make you rich.

I want to challenge you to leverage other people's hands, time, brains and technologies, to have synergy and power that can help you to be rich faster than most people.

To do this well, you must be social, open and friendly.

I laugh when people think I'm not "social" because I don't have social media account. But it's not like that. In fact, it's the opposite of that.

For example, how many of your Facebook's friends are truly your friends?

How many of them can you call today if you have any headache? How many of them truly care about you? How many of them can partner with you on any business project?

The truth is that, most "friends" on social media are non-friends.

Let me show you how to make real friends and form real partnership.

I was in a meeting in Abuja in February, 2018. During this meeting, different people from different parts of Nigeria talked about different things.

There among us was a very brilliant lady who happens to be a lawyer, with specialisation in business law.

Immediately after this over 5 hours' meeting, I asked myself, "Who can I connect with here?"

I thought about different people in that meeting and their contributions. My goal is to connect with just one or two people.

That lady seems to be the right person for me.

As we all moved out of the meeting venue, I approached her, "Hello, I like the way you talked. You these lawyers!", we both laughed and talked for some time then exchanged phone numbers.

Few hours after I landed in Lagos, I called her line. My goal is to build a business relationship with her, the way I've done with other people.

That's synergy. The more synergy you build, the more power you will have, the more wealth you can have.

I know a guy who is tech savvy. This guy knows so much about technologies, web designing, coding, programming etc.

These are skills highly needed to build a business in the 21 Century and I don't have them, non am I ready to spend time learning because I'm not having strength to be patient enough for anything as such.

What should I do?

I decided to partner with this guy and give him a percentage of my business.

That's exactly what I'm teaching all through this book.

You must believe in yourself but not in the wrong way.

You must not be a lone ranger or a perfectionist who want to do everything by himself. In fact, you must see yourself as a football coach, not a football player.

Your goal isn't to play ball. Your goal is to organize, train and motivate others to play the ball.

Your goal as an entrepreneur isn't to do it all. Your goal is to find people who can do it, employ them or partner with them, train them and motivate them.

This way, you can duplicate yourself into hundreds and thousands.

That's how great businesses are built and that's the only way you can build a business.

Whenever you meet someone who have strengths you need for your business, make sure you connect with them, very important, even if you don't have the money to engage or employ him/her now.

Form friendship. Form Partnership. Build synergy. Use other people's time, energy, strengths, brains to build wealth.

CHAPTER 3
USE THE TIME & ENERGY OF THE EMPLOYEES

This topic has been emphasized in this book but you can't hear it too often.

People get rich only by getting other people to work for them. There is no other way and I don't think it's unethical because most people actually are willing to sell their time for wages.

Since most people are willing and ready to sell their time for wage, and even think that's the only way to make money, it's only a good thing to buy their time and treat them better than they think possible.

If you're ever going to build a successful company, you must figure out how you can scale up your business, till a point where you cannot possibly manage your business by yourself.

Don't think like Bishop (in my earlier story) who thinks employing people means that he's giving them money. No. employing people is not giving them money. It's becoming richer.

I need to write this chapter because so many people are perfectionist who erroneously believe that other people cannot do their businesses like themselves.

That's rightly wrong.

It's right that someone else cannot do your business perfectly the way you can do it, but with appropriate training and retraining, you can get people to be 80% of you.

Yes, I know my Customers' Relation Manager (C.R.M) may not really handle our clients as "perfect" as I would, but after training, mistakes and few failures, he's now about 90% of me.

Similar thing happens with our customer care department and I need not to be a perfectionist or I'll not be able to build accompany that can give me the freedom I desire.

Don't be a perfectionist. Delegate authority and train people to do what you want to do.

Just as I'm writing these words, I heard my C.R.M saying a wrong thing to a client on phone. If I was a perfectionist, I'll feel like, "This guy isn't doing my work well. I'll do it myself". That's how so many people become slaves of their businesses.

Instead, I'm going to gently give this guy more training on what to say to clients on phone.

I repeat, don't be a perfectionist. Learn how to delegate duties and authority to people, even if they won't do it perfectly. Train and gently retrain them until they can become 70-90% as perfect as you can do it, so you can focus on other things that will help your business grow.

The time and energy of your employees is one of the greatest business assets you can ever have because those hands, time and energy can give you wealth and freedom.

The only caution you have to take is; employees are humans and deserve to be treated so.

I don't write this book to teach you how to "use" other people. Instead, I want to show you how to be at the right side of the money game.
While we all have options between being employees or being an entrepreneur and while none of those two choices is bad, I write this book for people who want to be on the right side of the game.

CHAPTER 4
USE THE HANDS OF THE ALREADY SUCCESSFUL BUSINESSES

Lumos is a company I like because of the creativity in the way they market their product which is renewable energy.

What Lumos did is simply to partner with the MTN Nigeria. By doing this, Lumos is able to leverage on the goodwill and network the MTN has built for more than one decade.

This happens all the time and you have to understand how it works because one of the hands you can use to be successful is the hands of the already successful business.

Yes, this may cost you something like a percentage of your business' profit or money, it does worth it at the long run.

In the year 1980, Bill Gates partner with IBM by allowing the IBM to use his operating system on their PC while he takes just a percentage on the PC's sales.

Before this time, IBM has become a mighty company while Microsoft was just a small company.

This leverage alone is what changed the life of Bill Gates.

Another type of leverage is what Naij did.

Naij.com is the most popular news blog in Nigeria (as at the time of writing this book), but it wasn't so until the year 2016/17 because Naij was just a new blog, but they were going to use the hand of an existing business and that was going to be the Facebook.

For the first three years or so, Naij ran massive adverts on Facebook and that helped them to build their brand and become the most popular news blog in Nigeria.

I know this method requires a lot of money but there's another cheaper example.

Woli Arole is the name of a Nigerian comedian who became popular via the Instagram.

What this guy does is that, he'll record his comedy with his smartphone and upload them on the Instagram. He later confessed on an interview that the social media is powerful.

Well, social media is only powerful for people who knows how to leverage on other people's businesses.

My company has four websites, a YouTube Channel and one social media account, as at the time of writing this book. At different degrees, all these websites, Channel & social media account are to help us get clients by leveraging on other successful businesses.

Take for instance, Google sends about 30,000 people to our websites every month without us having to pay for it. YouTube sends thousands of people to our videos for free and Facebook helps us to reach hundreds of people for free and hundreds of thousands on paid ads.

That's using the hands of the already successful companies.

My idea about life is; *use everything for your advantage. Be an opportunist and guild yourself from being used.*
If all you do is to consume other people's products, you're being used. If all you do is to consume other people's websites, you're being used.

While it's not possible for anyone of us to live without consuming other people's products and websites, we're being used if we don't think of creating saleable things that other people could consume as well.

Keep on thinking; what business can my business partner with? What business needs what my business is doing and how can we work together? How can I leverage on other successful companies, even if I'll have to pay them (e.g. in the case of advertising platforms like Facebook) to get my business successful.

You must keep on thinking, till you figure out how to use other people's hands, time and energy.

Stop trying to achieve success all by yourself. Leverage. Use other people's hands, time, brain and resources.

Stop being a lone ranger. Stop believing in yourself in a wrong way. Stop thinking you must do it all by yourself.

Partnering or working with a successful company can change your life completely. Be on the lookout for it.

CHAPTER 5
USING THE HANDS OF THE TECHNOLOGIES

I spent my first 11 years in a village where there was no electricity, not to talk of a TV set. Most children who grow up in cities get exposure to toys, TV and other small technologies but those were luxuries for village kids like myself.

Around year 2006/7 when everyone was crazy about social media, I was very reluctant, not because I was still a village guy but because I was working hard to be best student in my school plus, I always set goals to read 30-50 business/motivational books each year.

I was afraid of using the social media then, simply because I never wanted to be an average man. I wanted to be a great man and I knew wasting time on social media will not make that possible.

Not so much have changed since then. Till today, I'm still the village boy I was. I'm still so much "afraid" of technologies and using social media seems not for someone like me. Yes, I have no personal social media account!

But something has actually changed. While I remain a technology novice and "antisocial" (as one person called me), I've seriously fell in love with technologies, internet and the social media.

Though I don't know so much about technologies, I've worked hard to employ and partner with people who do. So, what I do is, whenever I have an idea or a problem I think any technology can help solve, I simply turn to my left or right hand side and speak with one of my team members.

In some cases, I have to call one or two of my business associates. This way, I can easily cover up my weakness in the area of technology know-how.

In the area of the internet (which happens to be the most powerful tool human beings ever created), just like a village boy, I'm not having any personal profile on any social media network.

But, I use social media extensively for business.

My company spent #2.2 million on Facebook ads last month alone and we've spent about #850,000 on Facebook ads this month.

As I write this book, we're working on a video ad that would be massively run on YouTube, Instagram, maybe Twitter and several other websites.

What Do I Want to Show You in This Chapter?

One of the most powerful hands you can use to make yourself rich in this Century is the hand of the technology.

Right from your phones, to your laptop, to the entire internet and hundreds of technologies in-between are great instruments you can leverage on to make yourself richer.

But, there's a problem. The problem is that, to truly leverage on the power of technology to build wealth, you must change your mind-set about what you think the technologies are for.

First, you must understand that every technology is someone's business and further use of it is also someone's business.

For example, Facebook isn't just a social media network but some people's business. In fact, Facebook is one of the 10 biggest businesses in the world.

While Facebook is a business, further use of it is patronizing a business because the more you use the Facebook, the more money you make for the Facebook owners. This is true with any other social media and websites you visit on the web.

Another good example is your phone. Your phone is a business for Apple, Samsung, Tecno or any company that made it. But that's not the whole story. The SIM card you bought, the recharge cards, the data, the websites you visit with the phone, etc. are all businesses for different people.

While I'm not angry for patronizing businesses, I love to see people patronizing my businesses too. Unfortunately, this has lead me to become an extremist as I try to see everything as a business tool.

You Don't Have to Be Like Me!

As for me, if I have to use the Facebook, Instagram, WhatsApp or any other social media, it must be strictly for business. If I need to communicate with my friends, I do so via phone calls or meet with them in the real life.

But you don't have to be like me. You can use the social media to network with your friends and family, only note that, the more you use social media and the internet for entertainment and socialization, the less you can use it for business.

Let me give you a simple law that will help you.

Each time you want to use the internet (for anything), kindly tell yourself, "I'm about to patronize someone's business" three times.

I think this should be helpful because, first, if you understand that EVERY website on the internet is someone's business, you'll be careful in the way you allow someone else's business to affect your life.

Second, I think this will also help you to want to create something that other people can patronize too.

5 Things to Do to Take the Advantage of The Technology.

First, **always remember that everywhere you go on the internet is someone's business** and every technology you use (e.g. your phone, TV set, Air Condition, etc.) is someone's business.

If you are aware of this fact, you'll be careful about the way you consume other people's business on the name of "entertainment". You'll also desire to use the technology to promote your own business.

The second thing I recommend you should do is to **go and design a website for your business**, immediately you get started. If you have a small business, consider having a website. If you're planning to start a business, let website be part of your marketing plans.

I was in a nice hotel in Abuja in February, 2018, only for me to know that this hotel doesn't have a website. While discussing the importance of the online presence with the hotel manager, he complained to me that the reason why they didn't have a website is because the business wasn't going fine. Well, the reason why the business isn't going fine maybe because they don't have a website and use other technologies.

My third recommendation; **You can start with your phone**. Maybe you have a small business and you don't think you can design a website now, simply start with your phone.

Make sure you have a data base of your clients or customers. Get the phone numbers of people who patronize your business, then use customized SMS (which is cheaper, yet improves your brand).

If you don't know about customized SMS before, search Google for "Customized SMS Portal in Nigeria (or your country)"

When you send a customized SMS to your clients or customers, they will receive it with your business name as sender.

For example let's assume that your business' name is Alex Ltd., when your customers receive your message, the sender will be Alex Ltd. This helps your brand.

Let's assume that you go out to shop and visited three supermarkets, Joe Supermarket, Ken Supermarket and Alex Supermarket. Few hours after you get home, you received an SMS from Alex "Thanks Mrs Rose, for patronizing us. Hope to see you another time".

If by next month you want to shop, which of the above three supermarkets are you likely to go?

The answer is simple, yet, it doesn't take you so much to use such simple technology.

How do you feel when you receive an SMS from your bank on your birthday?

It feels good yet, it doesn't cost your bank that much, just about #2 per SMS. You can use similar technology to promote your business.

My fourth recommendation for you is to actually **use social media**. Yes, use social media, but for your good.

I told you that I don't use social media, right? Wrong!

I'm one of the most influential people on Facebook and my team is working hard to duplicate the same thing for Instagram, YouTube, Twitter, etc.

There are so many people who are promoting their businesses via their personal profile on WhatsApp, Facebook, Instagram. While I think these people are doing well (compare to social media consumers), I think you could upgrade your game.

Yes, it's a great thing for you to promote your business via your personal social media accounts and I strongly recommend it, but be prepared to go bigger than that.

There are millions of consumers on the social media networks and it's your responsibility as an entrepreneur to promote whatever you're selling to them, in a big way.

My fifth recommendation; **Blog, if you can**.

Each time you go to Google to search for anything, know for sure that Google doesn't have any information. What Google does is to take you to someone else's blog and these blogs are making money.

Let me tell you how we do it in our company.

Because we have an Agric Technology company, we use the traffic Google gives us on our Agric related posts (which we have written on our blog), to get clients for our business.

What happens here is, thousands of people search the internet every month for keywords like, "Poultry farming", "Pig farming", "Fish farming", etc.

For those who search for these keywords in Nigeria, some of them are likely to land on our blog. From there, they will read about how our Agric consultancy services can help them.

After going through our blogs, some of these people can easily pay for our services and products (right there on the internet). Many of these transactions happen when I'm sleeping and that's what I call "Making money from other people's time & energy" because all these technologies (Blog, Google, Hosting and Domain Services used for our website, payment processor we use to collect money from our clients, etc.) were made by someone else.

Though we have to pay for a few of them, it's like someone gives you #100 and collects #1 back.

Let me give you another example which isn't mine.

A friend of mine knows about electrical works, fumigation, painting etc. but he didn't know how to get clients.

We then set up a website call Fumelect (you can see it at Fumelect.com). We designed the homepage of this website with the services my friend knows how to render and the next thing for us is to use a tool call "Google Keyword tool" (another technology you can search Google to know more about!) to know what people are searching for in relation to fumigation, electrical and painting business.

What we're going to do next is to write some articles in the areas of his services (electrical, fumigation, painting, etc.).

Though this may take us some time and efforts, few months to come when someone from Kano builds a house and needs the service of a painter, then go to the internet and type, "Good painter in Nigeria", he may get to my friend's website, read about his services and call him for his painting job.

Similar thing can happen for his fumigation, electrical and clearing services from Lagos, Imo, Abuja or any other city in Nigeria.

This is a level of "Using other people's energy". As time goes on, he can move to the next level. I'll explain.

If I'm the owner of a website that provides electrical, fumigation and painting services, after I've done all I explained above that allows me to use the "hands" of the technologies to get clients and make money, the next thing I'll do is to proceed to using the time and energy of other people.

As I've said earlier, there's nothing unethical about this. If at all anything, it's a righteous thing to do.

Let me give you some examples.

My company got a business in the year 2017 in Oyo, a town in Nigeria. I immediately called one of my guys to go and represent us and render the services.

This whole thing took him about 48 hours but I sent him #50,000. With his skills, that's similar to the amount many people in Nigeria earn in a month.

In this case, yes, I use his time and energy to render the service for my company's clients, but I also made him happy by paying him for 48 hours, what he should get for one month. Would you say this is unethical?

Second example.

My company as at the time of writing this book has more than 300 associates in more than 21 states of Nigeria and we work hard to increase this number day by day. These are the hands and potential hands for us to use.

But you know something? We're actually helping these guys to make money. So, the concept of using other people's time and energy is a nice thing to do.

Maybe you need one more example.

One day last year (2017), a guy came to my office, almost crying because he had no job. After taking my time to think about him, I thought he could be a good employee of my company so I employed him. Not just that, I actually decided to double his salary, compare to what he was collecting from his last job.

Today, this guy is the most valuable person in our company.

Yes, he uses his time and energy for the company, but we also helped him to get something better than what he was getting before.

Back to the example of my friend's electrical, fumigation and painting business.

After I've set up the website and start getting some clients, I'll immediately start employing people who could render such services.

So, my business model would look like;

Someone goes to Google to search for "Painters in Nigeria", gets to my blog to read about our services, gives us a call (which would be answered by a secretary), asks about our services and gets convinced.

After this man gives us his business, I or someone in my team will call an associates who is an experienced painter, to go and do the job. This way, we can have a project going on in Lagos, another in Abuja, another in Ghana, etc., with different people handling them.

If you look at the above business model very well, you'll see that it's easier for you to be rich, because you're using the "hands" of the technology and other people's time and energy.

This topic is about how you can use the "hands" of various technologies to promote your business and make you richer.

I've explained in details, how you can use the internet, blog, website, your phone, customized SMS, online payment processors etc. for your good.

The best thing you can take away from this chapter is; Stop seeing the internet or technologies as instruments of pleasure or entertainment.

Use your phone, the social media, the internet and every other technology to promote your business' brand.

My goal in writing this book is to show you how to use what you don't have for your advantage. It's called leverage and it's the power of the rich.

SECTION 56

Five Things Anyone Can Do To Become Rich – and just anyone can do them

In this section, I want to discuss with you five simple things anyone, I mean anyone on Earth, can do to become wealthy.

These five things I'm about to share with you are simple, yet effective, but most people will not do them.

The reason is because humans hate simplicity; we love things to be very complex.

We seem to believe that if a solution to our problem is not complex, it'll probably not work.

The following five simple things changed my life, and if you will try them, they will change yours too.

CHAPTER 1
DREAM BIG DREAM

I recall being one of the least performing students in a class of about 30 students during my junior high school years.

At that time I and a couple of other students in the class believed that the trio of Biodun, Taorid and Ponle were remarkably brilliant, the rest of us weren't.

We all believed none of us could be academically brilliant except for this trio. We depended on them during examinations, which unfortunately never worked for most of us.

Even after cheating on the trio during exams, we'd still find ourselves scoring poorly.

Now, something dramatic happened when we got to the Senior Secondary School One (the fourth year in high school in Nigeria).

The parents of these brilliant children withdrew them from our 'poor' school. Because they felt like their children's brilliance was beyond the school we attended (and they were right).

There we were, apparently nobody in my class to appear as the class leader, until one day myself and two others stood in front of our classroom.

We spoke about who would likely emerge as the new academic frontrunners in the class. "It is going to be me; I'm going to be the next leader of the class," I said, raising my hand.

What I said was so unrealistic that one of my friends laughed at me and said, "No! It cannot be you! It will be another person," he said, mentioning another's name.

I left that spot thinking "How can I become the next academic leader of my class?"

Now, I had a dream to pursue; I wanted to become the best, no longer one of the least performing students in the class.

Since I'd got a dream, I approached my father and told him a 'lie' to collect money then travelled to a neighbouring town to purchase different books. I bought books on Accounting, Commerce, and Economics. I began to study at night. I would wake up as early as 5.30am or 6.00 a.m and read for about an hour or two before going to school.

To abbreviate the long story, within six months, I became the best student in Commerce, Government, Economics, and Accounting and remained class 'king' till I left the high school. So many of my mates thought I was a genius but they were wrong.

I wasn't a genius. I was a dreamer.

So many people really don't understand the power in dreams; many don't understand what it means to say to oneself (and to believe) that you can do something.

Now, think about my situation back in high school. I had nothing, absolutely nothing! I was just a poor guy who also happened to be one of the dullest students in class.

However, because I dreamed and believed I became the best student in the class. It wasn't about me. It was about my dream.

Any other student in my class could have had a similar dream and emerged best the way I did.

This story has something to teach you.

It doesn't really matter who you are; what matters is your dream.

Today, if you take time to study the life of someone who is rich and successful, you'll discover that there are people who were born exactly like them, in almost similar circumstances, yet remain poor.

Today I'm richer than virtually anyone I grew up with, but you know something?

Everyone I grew up with was healthier than I was and some were born by richer parents.

What makes the difference?

Dreams! Dreams! Dreams!

Your life cannot be better than your dreams.

Now, if you want to change your life, then change your dreams.

Dream big and believe you can achieve it.

It doesn't matter how much you have (or don't have) today; dream of becoming successful, great, a millionaire.

Don't worry about how it will come to pass; just dream it. Meditate on it while in bed; shut your eyes and dream that you have become famous, rich, and successful.

Just dream it!

You might say: "Oh! Steve, this looks so abstract. What will happen when I dream it?"

What happens when people dream is; their subconscious assumes that they have actually got those things they dreamt.

Because of this, people who dream get their minds to desire what they dream. As this desire becomes stronger, they can't help but to take actions that will lead them to achieving those dreams.

The bigger your dream is, the more concentration you'll have in your life. The reason is because your mind will be "thirsty" and desirous of what you dream of every day.

Since age 15 when I began to dream, my life has been extremely focused and since then I watched an average of two movies a year and spent average of 30 minutes watching football in a year. In fact, I have never bought a TV set in my entire life.

"Boring life", some would say. But that's not true.

The reason most people think TV shows, football fixtures, movies and social media entertain them is because they really don't have big dreams.

As at the time of writing this book, I'm not on any social media platform and I'm happier and even more entertained than most people would.

If you dream big, your life will be focused; you'll be driven to study and read about people who have achieved what you want to achieve. It will push you to take actions that would make your life exciting, so much that you won't need so much TV entertainment.

Many Africans simply don't have meaningful dreams.

If you gather 100 African youths today and ask them what they want to become, their answer would more likely be, "I want to become successful".

Unfortunately, wanting to become 'successful' is not a dream.

"I want to become a millionaire by age 40" or "I want to become the greatest scientist in Africa by age 35" are better dreams.

Your dream must be specific.

Since clocking 15 years and as I grew, I could readily share my specific dreams no matter the time and place.

At age 15, my dream was to become the best student in the Commercial Department (class) of my high school; best student graduating student of all time at my polytechnic, at 18.

At age 20, it was to build a successful company. Today, my dream is to build a business empire and to change Africa by changing Africans' mind.

At every stage in my life, these dreams have kept me focused and 'crazy'.

I cannot live the way my peers live because I have dreams that keep me busy.

While many of my friends choose to spend 10 hours on social media or seven hours arguing about politics or even five 5 watching football matches on a weekly basis, I cannot.

The reason I cannot do all that is because I have big and exciting dreams, so exciting that I rarely feel the urge to be 'entertained' by anything else.

If you want to change your life, start dreaming big.

The most interesting thing about this is that, anyone can dream dreams. It doesn't matter what your situation is right now, you can start changing your life today if you begin to dream big.

This is a simple way to start.

Go right now to the internet and enter the word, "Beautiful Houses" into Google search. Look for the images of a very beautiful house you'll love to have at age 40, 50, 60, or an age next to your present age.

Do the same thing with cars. Get the images of your dream car, make coloured prints of them.

Paste these prints at your bedroom walls and stare at them day and night.

As you prepare to go to bed, shut your eyes and imagine your perfect future – driving luxurious cars and living in that exotic house.

See yourself in your company's annual general meeting; visit China, France, UK and US. Meet with the most important people in your country.

Read about yourself in national dailies; donate millions to the charity and build community clinics.

Shut your eyes and imagine doing all of these great things.

I assure you'll not be comfortable being poor when you wake up the next day, even if you're the poorest person in your country.

You'll be anxious to physically see everything you imagined.

You'll lose every appetite for time wasting activities and get busy looking for ways to achieve those dreams.

Don't trust me? Do this exercise every night for seven days and observe if your life will remain the same. If your mind, thoughts and actions remain same after such an exercise, then, I'm not the best business teacher in Africa (LOL).

The second thing you must do after you've started dreaming is to;

CHAPTER 2
SET EXCITING GOALS

In the year 1979, a group of researchers supposedly decided to study the lives of grandaunts of the Harvard Business School.

They wanted to know those who set goals and those that didn't. The study revealed that 84% didn't form the habit of setting goals, 13% set goals but don't make plans as to how to achieve their goals while 3% set goals and made plan as per how to achieve their goals.

Ten years later, the researchers tracked the sampled students to know how they were doing.

What the researchers found was baffling; 13% of students who were in the habit of setting goals went on to become two times richer than the 84% who didn't set goals.

The 3% who set goals and outline plans became ten times richer than the 84% who didn't set goals at all.

This is crazy, if you think about it.

But this wasn't the first study on the power of goal setting. In fact, there is a more famous study undertaken in 1953 by the Yale University.

In that study, 3% of the students who often set goals became richer than all the 97% combined who didn't set goals.

Whether goal setting is actually as powerful as being able to make someone ten times richer than those who don't set goals could be a subject of debate, but the power of goal setting in the life of a person cannot be underestimated.

I have actively set goals all my adult life and I can tell you the power of goal setting in a very simple sentence.

Goals help you to concentrate all your human resources and energy.

I really need you to understand this.

Goal setting doesn't have any magical power.

When God created mankind He did so with unusual power and strengths. We are capable of achieving unbelievable things which are evident in countless human inventions.

For instance, who could have imagined 200 years ago that humans could speak with each other from miles and miles away, talk less of one country to another. The telephone makes that possible and that is an evidence of human's brain's power.

Thanks to the inventor of television, who could have imagined in the last 150 years that we could beam audiovisual signals from, say, Kenya to South Africa?

Before the 20th Century, people believed that God didn't create humans to 'fly'.

The idea of an aeroplane looked so foolish that spiritual leaders of those days even preached against it as being sinful, "God created birds to fly, not men", they said.

Well, human brains are too powerful to be stopped by dogmas. Aircrafts were invented and today, we can fly.

Think about several human inventions and technological advancements and you'll agree with me that human brains are capable of performing miracles.

But wait!

We all have a problem and that's call distractions.

Because our brains are powerful, we easily get distracted into getting involve with too many things, the TV, the social media, the political news and arguments, the gossips, the pornographic musical videos, plus the complaints and the list goes on.

In this state of great distractions, no human being can achieve any significant success. Just as your eyes cannot see clearly except you focus on a single object, your brain cannot achieve success except you focus on a single mission.

What Goals Do To Your Brain

What goal setting does to your brain is actually very simple but powerful. It simply forces your brain to focus.

If you had the opportunity of entering my bedroom (sorry, you can't. Lol!), you'll see at least two papers on the wall, exactly in the direction I look the moment rise up from bed.

They are my current goals.

When I wake up in the morning and read my goals, it's hard for me to waste my day because my goals will give me focus.

Most failures in life occur because most people don't know where they are going. If you don't know where you're going, any bus is for you.

If you know where you're going, there's a specific car you're waiting for and a specific destination you're going.

The question is not whether or not you have the power to change your life. You obviously do. The question is would you take time to be focus, so that you can make use of the power within you?

The easiest way to remain focused is to set exciting goals for yourself.

I wake up each morning with excitement because I have exciting goals to pursue during my day. I go to my bed every night expecting the night to be short, so that I can get back to the day, to pursue my goals.

The reason is because I set exciting goals and I'm eager to see them coming to pass.

I want to build a great company. I want to also train at least one million Africans how to build their own companies. I want to change the continent of Africa by changing the way Africans think.

In fact, I sometimes consider myself the hope of Africa.

How could you have such great dreams and sleep nine hours a day? How can you have such great dreams and waste time on social media? How can you have such a great dream and waste time arguing football? How can you have such great goals and complain about what a government does or doesn't?

How can you have such lofty goals and not read good books or listen to good audio or video training every day, to be inspired and directed?

Setting exciting goals can change your life and anyone can do it.

So, How Do I Set Goals?

Now, these are three rules for goals setting;

Firstly, make it extremely simple.

Do not set a million goals or 100 goals; you don't need all that. Just make sure you set few goals, say, not more than 10.

I often set between 5 - 7 goals monthly.

Because my goals are very simple, I could easily read them with good knowledge of what they entail. Imagine 100 goals; way too much!

The second rule is to ensure your goals reflect different aspects of your life. Let it reflect your finances, marriage, spiritual life and possibly your health, too. To ensure clarity, you could pull out two goals for each area of your life.

The third rule about goal setting is to ensure your goals are specific. For instance, don't set goals to be wealthy by 2025. No! That's not a goal. Instead, set a goal to make X amount of money monthly by 2025.

Temptation of Dreaming Big

Another thing you want to run from is the temptation of dreaming big.

Though dreaming big is what you want to do, dreaming big could be tempting.

I recall dreaming of buying a Toyota Camry, 2008 model before I was 25, in spite only going fulltime into business six months after hitting age 21.

Although your intention might be to dream big, setting a goal to earn $1 million by next year, earning $500 currently on a monthly basis could soon discourage you.

Hence, you must believe in your goals to the extent that your mind conceives those goals.

Your goals must be big enough to make you feel excited just as your mind must see it as being achievable.

In his book, "Maximum Achievement," Brain Tracy shares the SMART goal setting formula.

S – Specific. Your goals must be specific (i.e. "I will make ₦1m a month", not "I'll be rich")

M – Measurable. You must be able to measure it (i.e. I set this goal last year. I now earn ₦300,000 monthly)

A – Achievable. Your mind must be able to conceive your goal's possibility.

R – Realistic. Setting a goal to run a marathon at 70 years may not be realistic.

T – Time-bound. You must specify when you expect to have achieved your goals.

I wish you find this formula useful.

After developing the habit of goal setting, be assured you've risen above the 84% of people (if judging by the 1979 study at the Harvard Business School).

The next thing you want to do is plan or strategise.

"I'm going to do ABC to pursue my goals"

"I'm going to read XYZ books to acquire more knowledge

and skills to enable me achieve my goals" "I'll stop doing

XYZ to enable me focus on my goals".

If you follow these simple steps – dream, set goals, plan and take action (even if you're the poorest person today) – you've become 'richer' than 97% of people in the world. It's only a matter of time before you'll be noticed at the top.

If you want your life to change, start by dreaming big; follow your dreams with goals and plans on how to achieve your goals and don't be a coward when it's time to take actions.

Anyone can do all these to change his or her life but only a few people will ever do it.

The third simple thing you can do to change your life today is;

CHAPTER 3
MAKE GOOD FRIENDS

I've written about this in the previous chapter and I have to repeat it here because of it importance.

There have been few times I experienced drastic changes in my life and one of such moments was in 2005/2006.

I had just been admitted into the polytechnic and (having set my eye on the top political position on campus) I was making so many friends.

This time however coincided with the period I read a book titled, "An Enemy Called Average" by John L. Manson.

In the book, I came across a quote: **"Your success or failure in the next five years will be determined by the books you read and the people you spend time with"**

Before then, I had discovered the power of reading good books so it was the segment about the sort of friends one associated with that got me thinking.

I began to list the names of my friends, asking, "With my knowledge of person XYZ, where's he likely to be in future; what is he likely to become in five years given his present lifestyle and habits?"

After this exercise, it became obvious to me that I was surrounded mostly by people who were going nowhere in life.

I knew I had to cut loose from such friends or end up like them. So, I made the decision to keep only three friends who I knew to be very serious.

Afterwards, I never made friends with unserious or negative people, rather, I surrounded myself with thinkers, readers and positive minded individuals.

These people challenge me, inspire me, share books they read with me, and accelerate my achieving the goals I set – one of the reasons this book was written.

I'll probably be an average person today if I hadn't surrounded myself with such people.

I suggest you do a similar exercise if you desire to achieve success in life.

Why Do We Become Like People We Spend Time With?

We are a reflection of those we spend most time with because attitudes and habits are as contagious as having a cough or other contagious diseases.

Our attitude is similar to laughing. When you see or hear someone laughing, you're likely to laugh. In a less obvious way, you're likely to dream big, if you spend time with people who dream big.

One of the simplest things you could do if you desire to change your life today is to change your associates and people you spend time with.

One of the things responsible for my accelerated success is my being constantly on the look out to meeting and associating with great minds.

If you ask me to choose between having $1m and having great friends, I'll choose the latter because great friends are worth far more than all the money in the world.

So, again, review your associates if you desire to make meaningful impact in your life. Stop associating with persons with negative influence. Stop sitting with people who only complain. Stop discussing with people who don't believe in their countries or continent.

The more time you spend with negative and average people, the more negative and average you'll become. You must make conscious effort to become friends with great minds.

How Do You Know Great Minds?

You shall know them by their words.

Great people don't complain. Great people don't spend their entire time arguing about pedestrian stuffs like politics or football.

They don't blame anyone but self for their poverty or failures; they consider themselves agents of change, not victims of circumstances.

Take the pains to make friends with great persons when you hear them speak.

Don't misunderstand me; I don't refer to the richest person in Africa when I refer to 'great minds', because people aren't 'great' as a result of their money or fame; but by the quality of their thoughts.

In other words, you don't have to have richest man in your city on your friends list; but consciously dissociating from negative influences and associating with goal getters who will be a constant source of inspiration.

How Do You Keep Great Friends?

Water the friendship just as you'll do a seed.

Put calls through quite often and create time to visit, when possible. It's not enough to 'Like' Facebook posts of your friends or chat on WhatsApp. So, create opportunity for physical exchanges and meetings as often as possible.

As you do all these, ensure you don't make friends for the wrong reasons. Don't be selfish, be generous and prepared to offer something in return.

This is my last advice here; become who you want your friends to be.

As a matter of law, humans don't fancy associating with persons or groups with whom they don't share similar values.

It doesn't matter how much you try, great minds will distance themselves from you if you choose to remain negative.

For instance, if you don't make effort to read good books, people who do will dissociate from you because you probably cannot engage in quality discussions with them.

Like minds attract. If you strive towards greatness, such people will be attracted to you. However, if you choose to remain 'little' in life, persons who desire greatness will detest being your friends.

So, remember: If you want to be great, associate with great minds.

CHAPTER 4
SEEK KNOWLEDGE

About the age of 20, I saw a man reading in front of his house as I made my way to church one evening. As it was my custom, I moved closer, greeted him and admired the book he was reading with the intent to borrow it (which I succeeded in doing).

That book completely changed the trajectory of my life. It did not only make me a new person, but also an inspiration to many young people and a 'rebel' to the conservatives.

In November, 2008, though I was broke, I wanted to start a business. So, I travelled to Lagos (Nigeria) to meet with a sister with the hope of raising some funds. Returning home, she and her husband gave me about ₦8,000.

I stopped at the CMS, Lagos where I spent almost the entire money purchasing books.

By the time I returned to Osun State I had a bag filled with books and only ₦500 left. "But you told me you needed capital to start a business?" my lovely mum said, after an embrace.

"These are the capital I need for now," I said, pointing to the bag containing the books.

I quickly set out to reading these books.

One book that I took special note of was entitled, "You Can Negotiate Anything" written by Herb Cohen.

Three weeks after reading this small book, I successfully negotiated and secured the capital I sought.

In the year 2014, I came across a $7 book on the World Wide Web, and convinced it had lessons to teach, I ordered for the book which was shipped to me from the California, US.

I hadn't read to page 12 when I discovered a principle for doubling my company's revenue.

Sometime in February, 2018, I visited YouTube for educational purposes, as I often do after the day's task to learn from my many business teachers.

And there I was learning from one of my teachers (who don't even know I exist). He spoke extensively about how to lead, making reference to an employees' management software.

At the time, this piece of information was worth ₦1 million to me because I had difficulty in this area as my business grows.

Why Am I Telling You All These Personal Stories?

One of the fastest ways to change your life is to change what you read.

No doubt, everyone reads. But, what sort of materials do you read - Facebook posts, Twitter noise and Gossips?

Do you read books or watch video depicting people who have achieved greatness in life?

What you read is who you are. Who you are is what you have. If you want to have some things you don't have now, you must change who you are now.

If you want to change who you are, simply change what you read.

Above are few of my personal stories which I thought I should share with you. I have read almost every motivational book I came across since I was 18 years.

I can attest that my life has been transformed hundreds of times over and each made me better and richer.

It's rather unfortunate many Africans hate to read.

An average African doesn't read except recommended academic texts, company-related materials and the social media posts.

I don't understand why everyone seems not to know the reason for our poverty.

You can't be a rich man with a poor mind and you can't have a rich mind, until you read and listen to rich thoughts.

You want to be successful and rich?

Read or watch videos of the rich and successful people, every day of your life.

If you want to build a successful company, for example, and you decide to spend just 30 minutes every day reading books or listening to audio or video tapes from people who have built successful company before, I don't know anything in the natural realm of man that can stop you from building a successful company.

The reason why most people think they need a government to help them is because they have weak minds, minds that have not been built with knowledge.

Almost everyone was amazed by my courage when I was going to the business world. In fact, my family members thought I was foolish or getting mad because they were expecting me to live a normal life of "get good grades and good jobs".

What these people didn't know was that I've read from more than 250 books and with such knowledge, nothing in the realm of man can stop me, not even a bad economy or a bad government.

I told myself, "I will rather die than to be a poor man".

How Do I Find Good Books to Read?

The excuse I often get whenever I criticise fellow Africans for reading the 'wrong' set of books or materials is, "I don't know where to get good books".

Well, the reason you don't know is because you don't genuinely desire it, hence you won't even bother to search for it.

I know bookstores and libraries in almost every city I've visited because I care about reading good books and I'll make effort to search for them, even if I'll have to travel miles.

You'll always know how to get whatever you truly desire.

Here are some things you can do now to discover good books;

Search the Google for the phrase, 'Book stores in Lagos,' or any other city you live.

Visit the physical or virtual store of your desired store and buy one or two books.

You could also input, "The best business or financial books" into Google.

Write down the titles that catch your fancy and search for the Portable Document File (PDF) format of the titles. Quite often, PDF or e-books (as they sometimes referred to) are free to download.

Also, they are sometimes available for free on YouTube as audio books; download and listen to them daily.

In addition, search, download and listen to speeches and interviews of some successful people you know.

Search YouTube for videos discussing "How to be a successful business person", "How to market my business ideas" and any other subjects you wish to learn. Others may include subjects such as leadership, public speaking, human relationship and marketing. I'm certain you'll come across several business teachers if you search Google and YouTube.

Take these teachers as seriously as you took your mathematics teachers, for instance; 'consume' many other materials you discover on the web and don't let a day pass you by without learning from at least one of these success stories.

Use the internet, especially sites and platforms like Google and YouTube to continuously learn.

That's what I do and I recommend you do same.

I've spent the last one decade studying the lives of great people – Nelson Mandela, Bill Gates, Obafemi Awolowo, Ghandi, Bill Clinton, Warren Buffet, amongst others – in a numerous facets of life.

Though these people are different in so many ways, one thing they have in common is the fact that they either are or were vicious and eclectic readers.

It's smarter to read a thing or two about marathoners if you intend to attempt a mile in four minutes else you'll waste so much of your time.

If you want to climb the tallest mountain in the world, you'd better take time to learn from professional climbers.

Likewise, if you want to be rich and successful, you must learn every day from the rich and successful otherwise you could remain poor for the rest of your life.

The fifth thing I think anyone can do is;

CHAPTER 5
START A BUSINESS

I challenged you in the previous chapter to become an inquisitive student of business and acquire knowledge every day of your life because this is the only way you'll ever become incredibly successful.

But, what happens after acquiring so much knowledge? What happens after reading through this book?

Knowledge Isn't Power.

In the past, so many people have said 'knowledge is power', but on the contrary, I think action is power. It doesn't really matter how much you know, what matters is taking actions.

While taking action without knowledge leads you to failure, acquiring knowledge without actions leads you to failure as well.

The good news is that almost anyone can take actions. Yes, anybody can start a business.

I mean, except you have some very critical health challenges, you can start a business. In other words, you have almost every other thing you need to start a business once you're healthy.

> But why can't most people start their own business?

There are three problems most people encounter when they think of starting abusiness.

First, they never acquired the requisite skills to run a business and make it successful.

Imagine someone who has spent his entire adulthood as an employee, but somewhere along the line he or she suddenly wishes to start his own business.

It is important to understand that what it takes to succeed as an entrepreneur is entirely different from what it required as an employee.

Just imagine a 40-year-old man who has been a footballer since he was 18 years old but decides to begin a professional wrestling career.

Though possible, he can't do it without serious practice and almost completely changing his ways of thinking. The reason is because, what footballers do on the pitch is quite different from what wrestlers do. The way a wrestler's brain is wired is quite different from the way a footballer reasons.

Also, footballers are trained to use their legs more often, but wrestlers use their hands.

Since these two professions are very different, a 40-year-old footballer must take time to learn, practice and change his thinking if he truly wishes to succeed as a wrestler.

Sadly, many people who want to migrate from being employees to being entrepreneurs are not prepared to learn daily and change their orientation.

Most people who start businesses in Africa still think as employees, which is the very reason they won't succeed or take-off in the first instance.

The second reason why many Africans can't start a business is because they wish they could have a predictable map of how it would turn out.

In February 2018, I was invited to speak in the University College Hospital, Ibadan and I had to engage some young doctors in a discussion where they sought to know what business idea they could pursue to make them successful.

It wasn't surprising because I frequently received emails with such questions. Well, there's no such business!

I ignore mails with the question: "Please what business could I start with X amount of money to earn X amount after six months".

You can be almost sure a boy could acquire good grades if he studied very hard. You can be almost sure a man could get a good job and earn good wages, but that's not business because there's no predictable map in the business world.

No business can promise you a predictable outcome!

You'll probably wait forever if you're waiting on a predictable map to the business world because nothing of sort exists under the Sun.

So many people are confused (just as everyone who wants to start a business is confused) about which business to start to make them huge money.

Well, you have to stop expecting that predictable map because it doesn't exist.

This is the reason I have preached faith earlier inside this book. The only assurance you have as an entrepreneur is the faith in yourself.

The only assurance I can give you is the plausibility of succeeding and achieving riches if you have courage to start a business and learn every day of your life.

Don't wait for any guarantee because no business comes with such.

People who want guarantee before they get started in the business world think business is about what you sell, but they are wrong because business is not about what you sell but **how you sell what you sell.**

Your success in business doesn't depend on what you do, but **how you do what you do.**

That's the reason why it's ignorance for anyone to tell you; "If you go into the XYZ business you're going to make millions". No. You're not going to make any money in the XYZ business. You're only going to make money IN THE WAY you run the XYZ business.

If people become successful by engaging in particular businesses, it would have been possible to predict, say, 'you'll make millions if you sell soap', but there's nothing like that.

See these examples;

Aliko Dangote has become a billionaire by selling cement even though there are thousands of people who sell cement and make no money.

Mark Zuckerberg became a billionaire by creating a social media platform but there are many who have created similar sites and make no money.

Apple has sold phones and computers to become the most valuable company in the world in an industry where many others are also engaged with no success.

DO YOU GET MY POINT NOW?

Individuals don't become successful businessmen because of what they do, but because of **how they do what they do.**

To think you'll succeed if you sell XYZ is to give the impression you don't understand how business works.

You cannot become rich by what you sell. You can only become rich by HOW you sell what you sell.

That's the reason why if you give 100 people the same amount of money to go and start the exact same business today, in the next two years, more than 90 of them must have failed or just struggling. The top 3 who are doing well are not doing well because of the business they are doing (because all of them are doing the same business), but because of HOW they are doing the business they are doing.

WHAT IS THE LESSON HERE?

Stop waiting for that predictable business idea that can make you millions because it does not exist.

Instead, learn how to discover lucrative business opportunities with the formulas I shared with you in the second section of this book.

WHAT IF I CAN'T DISCOVER A BUSINESS OPPORTUNITY OR I DON'T HAVE MONEY?

Start with whatever your mind can find, with whatever you have. Keep on learning and practicing.

My story is the best weapon I can use to show you how this works.

It all started when I was 13. I wondered why everyone wants to be employee.

I didn't know anything about business when I started my first business at age 15. I just loved making money and the whole thing looked like a game, so I loved it.

The business I started at 15 lacked any business strategy. I just did what my mind could find. I bought a bicycle and started a bicycle renting business which I ran after school and at the weekends and holidays.

The business model was very simple. My mates would follow me to an open field where they would pay me #10 to ride my bicycle for 10 minutes or #20 to ride my bicycle for 20 minutes.

After about one year of doing this, I sold my bicycle and what else can I start? I simply started the business I've learned from my step-brother, photography.

I bought a simple camera and started taking the pictures of my school mates while they paid me #50 per photograph.

I did some investing between my age 17-20 and at 21 and six months when I was going fully into the business world, though "well" prepared after reading from close to 250 books, I still didn't know what business to start nor did I have money, except #8,500.

Someone I knew I just had to start, anyhow.

It was the era of mobile telecommunication boom in Nigeria and all I had to do was what my mind could find, even though I knew it's not that "million dollar" business idea I needed.

My first day profit (which wasn't a profit at all) was #5 and I smiled over it.

I later discovered a special snacks business brought to Nigeria by some Ghanaians and I wanted to use the knowledge I've acquired through hundreds of books to build a snackscompany around that.

I spent some years trying and learning.

From there, I started a blog, where I wrote my business experiences to teach others.

I kept on trying, learning and making mistakes, until one very night when I was preparing to sleep, from nowhere I can't explain, an idea flashed through my mind.

It was to build an Agric technology company.

Somehow I knew that was what I've been waiting for. You cannot sleep in a night like that so I kept on writing and thinking almost all night. It was Friday and by Saturday morning, I went to meet one of my friends I needed to get started with implementing my new business idea, even though I still didn't have money.

I leveraged on my blog to get clients for my new business idea and tried to negotiate with few of my friends.

Unlike how it has been happening before, this time around, people around me were willing to support my idea (because it was obviously a great one). I just needed to speak to about three people among which one of them was willing to invest three million Naira and another, about one million Naira.

It was so nice that I only accepted the first man and found a way to reject the second man.

With three million Naira, my blog giving us some clients already and my wife as my first employee, we had more power to grow fast.

Till the time of writing this book, we're yet to build 50% of what that single idea has for us.

We now have networks in more than 25 states of Nigeria, hoping to dominate Nigeria in the next two years and try to dominate Africa soon.

I'M SURE MY STORY SHOWS YOU WHAT THIS CHAPTER IS ALL ABOUT

You don't have any excuse. You may not have money and that's fine. You may not have that "million dollar" idea yet and that's fine.

But, you can start from where you are, with what you have, using the wisdom you've gotten from this book and keep on learning.

Understanding that you can never become rich, until you build an empire that allows you to use other people's brains, time and energy is very important. That's the first chapter in this book.

Believing that money is plenty (and NOT scarce) is very important, so that you'll be able to dream big. That's one of the things I shared with you in the first section.

Looking for change, problems, people, knowledge and riches is very important for you to discover the hidden business opportunities and that's what I shared with you in the section two.

Concentrating on building your own wealth requires that you stop looking at your background, the political leaders, the "better" countries and the poverty. That's section three.

Knowing that everything you have and every hands you can get are for your use, from your friends, to your employees, your partners, already successful businesses, etc. and always forming synergy, partnership and using what you don't have is very important, asdiscussed in section four of this book.

Section five of this book is to prepare your mind-set as you're getting started in the business world. The analogy about turbulence as aeroplane take-off and the story of the Chinese bamboo is to let you know that, the beginning isn't likely to be easy for you (because it's not easy for anyone), not because you're in Africa or because of witches.

It's as normal as the Rain and the Sun. My story already tells you that.

I "preached" faith because that's the only asset you can ever have. You must believe in yourself or else, you'll be discouraged when things are not working (as they will many time be).

This last section is to drive you to action. You must dream big dreams, set exciting goals, stay focus, seek business and financial knowledge, every day of your life and take actions.

Don't tell me it's not easy because I never promised you it's going to be easy. Life is about eating the ugly frogs.

Life is about sacrificing today because of tomorrow.

Life is about being a warrior when everyone is a civilian.

Life is about fighting for freedom.

Life is about smiling when you fail, because you know that you're going to succeed eventually.

Life is about doing what your age mates don't want to do today, so that you'll have what they cannot have tomorrow.

Please make sure you read this book at least three times, so that you can get the best out of it.

I want to leave you with the following 52 quotations, to keep you going, every week of the year.

1.   "You don't learn to walk by following rules. You learn by doing, and by falling over" ~ **Richard Branson. Founder Virgin Group**

2.   "If you don't sell, it's not the product that's wrong, it's you" ~ **Estee Lauder. Co-Founder, Estee Lauder**

3.   "It's important to be willing to make mistakes. The worst thing that can happen is you become memorable."
~**Sara Blakely Founder, Spanx, inc**

4. *"Don't ever let someone tell you that you can't do something. Not even me"*
~Chris Gardner. Founder Gardner Rich & Co.

5. "Your work is going to fill a large part of your life, and the only way to be truly satisfied is to do what you believe is great work. And the only way to do great work is to love what you do." **–Steve Jobs, Co-Founder, Chairman and CEO, Apple**

6. "It's almost always harder to raise capital than you thought it would be, and it always takes longer. So plan for that." **–Richard Harroch, Venture Capitalist and Author**

7. "Don't worry about failure; you only have to be right once." **–Drew Houston, Dropbox Co-Founder and CEO**

8. "If you are not embarrassed by the first version of your product, you've launched too late." **–Reid Hoffman, LinkedIn Co-Founder and Venture Capitalist**

9. "I knew that if I failed I wouldn't regret that, but I knew the one thing I might regret is not trying." **– Jeff Bezos, Amazon Founder and CEO**

10. "The way to get started is to quit talking and start doing." **–Walt Disney, Co-Founder, Disney**

215

11.   "What do you need to start a business? Three simple things: know your product better than anyone, know your customer, and have a burning desire to succeed." **–Dave Thomas, Founder, Wendy's**

12.   "As long as you're going to be thinking anyway, think big." **–Donald Trump, The Trump Organization President**

13.   "Don't be afraid to assert yourself, have confidence in your abilities, and don't let the bastards get you down." **–Michael Bloomberg, Former Mayor of New York and Founder of Bloomberg L.P.**

14.   "If you're not a risk taker, you should get the hell out of business." **–Ray Kroc, McDonald's Founder**

15.   "The secret of getting ahead is getting started. The secret of getting started is breaking your complex overwhelming tasks into smaller manageable tasks, and then starting on the first one." **–Mark Twain, American Humorist and Author**

16. "If you just work on stuff that you like and you're passionate about, you don't have to have a master plan with how things will play out." **–Mark Zuckerberg, Facebook Founder and CEO**

17. "Wonder what your customer really wants? Ask. Don't tell." **–Lisa Stone, BlogHer Co-Founder and CEO**

18. "When you find an idea that you just can't stop thinking about, that's probably a good one to pursue." **–Josh James, Omniture CEO and Co-Founder**

19. "Waiting for perfection is never as smart as making progress." **–Seth Godin, Author**

20. "Every worthwhile accomplishment, big or little, has its stages of drudgery and triumph: a beginning, a struggle and a victory." **–Mahatma Gandhi, Political and Spiritual Leader**

21. "I'm convinced that about half of what separates the successful entrepreneurs from the non-successful ones is pure perseverance." **–Steve Jobs, Co- Founder and CEO, Apple**

22. "I cannot give you the formula for success, but I can give you the formula for failure--It is: Try to please everybody." -- **Herbert Bayard Swope**

23. "Success is not the key to happiness. Happiness is the key to success. If you love what you are doing, you will be successful." -- **Albert Schweitzer**

24. "A successful man is one who can lay a firm foundation with the bricks that other throw at him." -- **David Brinkley**

25. "In order to succeed, your desire for success should be greater than your fear of failure." -- **Bill Cosby**

26. "In order to succeed, we must first believe that we can." -- **Nikos Kazantzakis**

27. "Many of life's failures are people who did not realize how close they were to success when they gave up." -- **Thomas Edison**

28. "Don't be distracted by criticism. Remember-- the only taste of success some people get is to take a bite out of you." -- **Zig Ziglar**

29. "The secret of success is to do the common thing uncommonly well." -- **John D. Rockefeller Jr.**

30. "There is a powerful driving force inside every human being that, once unleashed, can make any vision, dream, or desire a reality." – **Anthony Robbins**

31. "The secret to success is to know something nobody else knows." -- **Aristotle Onassis**

32. *"I never did anything worth doing by accident, nor did any of my inventions come indirectly through accident, except the phonograph. No, when I have fully decided that a result is worth getting, I go about it, and make trial after trial, until it comes."* -- **Thomas Edison**

33. *"The only place where success comes before work is in the dictionary."* -- **Vidal Sassoon**

34. *"Keep on going, and the chances are that you will stumble on something, perhaps when you are least expecting it. I never heard of anyone ever stumbling on something sitting down."* -- **Charles F. Kettering**

35. "The world changes constantly, and so does business. The only thing that remains the same is your innate abilities." — **David Weber**

36. "People get good gigs because they stand up You don't get picked. Reject the tyranny of picked. Pick yourself." ~**Seth Godin**

37. "If you can raise a family, then you can build a business." - **Michael Port**

38. "If the door to your dreams is locked, Kick It Open" - **Kevin Jimeno**

39. "When defeat comes, accept it as a signal that your plans are not sound, rebuild those plans, and set sail once more toward your coveted goal. If you give up before your goal has been reached, you are a "quitter." A quitter neverwins, and a winner never quits."-- **Napoleon Hill**

40. "Generate so much loving energy that people want to just come and hang outwith you. And when they show up, bill them!" **-Stuart Wilde**

41. "Anyone who stops learning is old, whether at twenty or eighty. Anyone whokeeps learning stays young. The greatest thing in life is to keep your mind young." ~ **Henry Ford**

42. "Hope and fear cannot occupy the same space. Invite one to stay".
~ Maya Angelou

43. "Friends who don't help you climb, will want you to crawl right next to them.Choose your closest people carefully." **-Julie Melillo**

44. "Begin challenging your own assumptions. Your assumptions are your windows on the world. Scrub them off every once in a while, or the light won'tcome in." -- **Alan Alda**

45. You have to take risks. As far as achieving success in business, here is a quoteto live by: "You miss 100% of the shots you never take." **Wayne Gretzky**

46. "We can't solve problems by using the same kind of thinking we usedwhen we created them." **Albert Einstein**

47. "When you innovate, you've got to be prepared for people telling you that youare nuts," **Larry Ellison, the founder of Oracle.**

48. "Never give up. Today is hard, tomorrow will be worse, but the day aftertomorrow will be sunshine," **Jack Ma, the founder of the Chinese ecommerce megaloth Alibaba.**

49. "The Pessimist Sees Difficulty In Every Opportunity. The Optimist SeesOpportunity In Every Difficulty." -**Winston Churchill**

50. "People Who Are Crazy Enough To Think They Can Change The World, AreThe Ones Who Do."- **Rob Siltanen**

51. "The Only Limit To Our Realization Of Tomorrow Will Be Our Doubts OfToday."- **Franklin D. Roosevelt**

52. "It's Not Whether You Get Knocked Down, It's Whether You Get Up." – **VinceLombardi**

www.ingramcontent.com/pod-product-compliance
Lightning Source LLC
Chambersburg PA
CBHW031532210526
45464CB00020B/1635